boutique
wedding cakes

boutique
wedding cakes

bake and decorate beautiful cakes at home

Victoria Glass

photography by Laura Forrester

LONDON · NEW YORK

Designers Luis Peral and Barbara Zuñiga
Editor Rebecca Woods
Head of Production Patricia Harrington
Art Director Leslie Harrington
Editorial Director Julia Charles

Stylists Luis Peral and Victoria Glass
Indexer Hilary Bird

First published in 2012
by **Ryland Peters & Small**
20–21 Jockey's Fields
London WC1R 4BW
and
519 Broadway, 5th Floor
New York, NY 10012

www.rylandpeters.com

10 9 8 7 6 5 4 3 2 1

Text © Victoria Glass 2012

Design and photographs
© Ryland Peters & Small 2012

ISBN 978 1 84975 263 3

A catalogue record for this book is available from the
British Library.

US Library of Congress cataloging-in-publication data
has been applied for.

Printed in China

• All spoon measurements are level unless otherwise specified.
• Use either metric or imperial/cup measurements, do not use a
combination of both.
• All eggs are large (UK) or extra large (US), unless otherwise specified.
It is recommended that free-range, organic eggs be used whenever possible.
• Ovens should be preheated to the specified temperatures. All ovens work
slightly differently. We recommend using an oven thermometer and suggest
you consult the maker's handbook for any special instructions, particularly
if you are cooking in a fan-assisted/convection oven, as you will need
to adjust temperatures according to the manufacturer's instructions
• Philadelphia (full-fat, not the reduced fat variety) has been specified for
icings as this is the only brand I have found which doesn't turn to liquid
when whisked with an electric hand whisk.

contents

essential recipes & techniques 19

classic elegance 37

chic & sophisticated 65

a splash of colour 89

changing seasons 119

introduction

The wedding cake offers you the perfect opportunity to showcase the style and personality of the couple it's celebrating, whether that's bold and distinctive, classic and elegant or a reflection of the bride and groom's personal obsession with the family tartan. Whatever design path you choose, you can always throw a few surprises into the mix. This book provides you with a deliciously varied and exciting range of flavours, from timeless sponges to indulgent and unique combinations. All recipes include quantity charts for different sized and shaped pans at the back of the book. This means that you can pick and choose both the flavours and size of your cakes to suit your taste, as well as use the cake recipes for other occasions once the wedding cake has been baked, decorated, sliced and, finally, eaten.

The cake is an important focal point at a wedding reception, creating an eye-catching centrepiece for the day. But just because a wedding cake, with all its weighty symbolism of union, prosperity and fertility, is traditional, it doesn't mean the design or flavour has to be.

I have carefully paired each showcased design with a different and fitting recipe, but these pairings are merely suggestions. There is absolutely no reason to follow my lead. In fact, I actively encourage you to forge your own flavour path and pick and choose recipes according to your own taste and considerations. Light, citrusy notes may be preferable for a date in the middle of June, whereas an indulgent Black Forest cake can work wonders to warm the chill of a cold, November night.

Personally, I always favour serving the cake as dessert as it is the perfect way to be both economical and indulgent. So often, the cake gets cut and wheeled out at about 10 o'clock, when guests have already eaten a three-course meal and drunk enough champagne to launch a fleet. This way, your guests won't be too stuffed to eat it and your delicious efforts are guaranteed to be better remembered, as well as enjoyed. If, on the other hand, the cake is going to be served late in the evening with coffee, make a note of the dessert choice to avoid any flavour repetition – a lemon cake will seem less enticing after a lemon tart.

You needn't feel that you should stick to just one recipe – the bride and groom may have incompatible tastes when it comes to cake and you may need to cater for specific dietary requirements. Whatever the reason for opting for more than one cake flavour, be it necessity, gluttony or indecision, guests will certainly be grateful to be offered a choice.

Years ago, I made a wedding cake in the under-equipped kitchen of a holiday rental cottage as a gift for a friend. I had brought my own pans, rolling pin and piping nozzles, but nothing else. I had no measuring scales, electric whisks or spatulas and had to mix the cake batter in a saucepan, as the cottage didn't have a single mixing bowl. The only measuring tools I had were a couple of tablespoons, teaspoons and a vintage Pyrex jug. Although this situation could never be described as ideal, it certainly proved to me that you don't need state-of-the-art facilities to get the job done and done well. Although flashy electric mixers and digital scales will always make the job easier and quicker, you'll be amazed at what can be achieved with little or no expensive or specialized tools. Specific equipment is needed for some of the cake designs in this book, but others require little more than what you'll find already in the back of your kitchen cupboards. If you honestly assess your own levels of skill and confidence before starting your cake, you shouldn't find too many bumps in the road. An optimistic, gung-ho spirit will serve you just as well as any fashionable kitchen gadgets.

Now, deep breath, shoulders back, and pop on your pinny. You're about to make an exquisitely beautiful and delicious wedding cake.

how to use this book

My aim is to de-mystify tricks of the trade and help guide you, while avoiding being too prescriptive. Although I offer you design and flavour pairings, there is still plenty of room for the cake you create to reflect your personal creativity. This is especially important to bear in mind should anything not go entirely to plan. If your icing skills aren't quite as flawless as you had hoped, or your sugar flowers not quite as neat as nature's, there is no need to feel deflated or disappointed in yourself. For the best results, follow my guide to assessing the kind of baker you are on pages 10–11, so that you can steer away from any projects that may lead to a nervous breakdown. Everyone is different. We approach work differently, set differing timetables and deal with stress differently, so just work out what fits you best. The more you enjoy working on this project, the more likely you are to succeed and be proud of the results.

I have carefully paired each cake design with a flavour that appropriately reflects the style. Colourful, feminine designs, perfect for spring and summer, have been matched with light and fresh flavours; Jade Garden makes a perfect marriage with orange and polenta cake, while Brighton Rock is an ideal match for peanut butter and chocolate chip's nostalgic and genial charm. I have paired formal cakes with classic flavours, and designs best suited to autumn or winter and evening receptions with richer confections. Designs coated with indulgent chocolate instead of sugar paste naturally lend themselves to dessert, so I have paired them with cakes which make for particularly delicious desserts. Midnight Lotus is matched with a gloriously decadent chocolate rum truffle torte and Royal Ballet's white chocolate and cardamom cake makes a delicious end to any meal.

Each pairing gives the recipe for a single tier in a specific size on the main page, with a variety of quantities and oven times for alternative sized cakes and shapes at the back of the book. Although the recipe shows only the ingredients quantities for a single tier, the decorating ingredients are given for all three tiers. Please bear in mind that these quantities are approximates only, as the amount of sugar flowers or chocolate decorations you will need will depend on the size of the cakes you make, and so it follows that the quantity of floristry paste, sugar paste or modelling chocolate used for decorations is also dependent on cake size. There is a chart for working out the quantities for all cake and cake drum coverings at the back of the book, so you will know exactly how much sugarpaste, modelling chocolate or marzipan you will need to cover the cake sizes and shapes you have chosen.

A few notes on baking... Please do not mix and match with the measurements for metric and imperial. Choose either metric (grams) or imperial (ounces and cups) for the best results. I would advise against making enough cake mixture for all three (or more, if you wish) tiers in one go. You will struggle to fit in the sheer volume of cake batter in most mixing bowls and the arms of most electric whisks will be too short to reach the bottom of the mixture, without creating an awful mess. You may also find that you have only enough oven space for specific sized cakes at a time, so pop your empty cake pans in a cold oven before you begin, to work out the most sensible use of your space and time. Prepared cake batter should not be left to sit about in a bowl while the rest is cooking – it must be cooked immediately or the raising agents will start working before it is baked and affect the rise.

You can, of course, choose to make more than one flavour. Simply find the recipes with methods on the main pages and follow the ingredients charts at the back for your desired cake pan sizes. For example, you could follow the recipe for a 15-cm/6-inch fruit-cake, a 20-cm/8-inch chocolate fudge cake and a 25-cm/10-inch green tea cake. There is a guide in the back of the book for working out portion numbers, so you can calculate the cake size you will need to make for the number of guests you are catering for.

All the recipes for essential cake decorating can be found at the front of the book for ease, so that everything you need to keep coming back to, such as royal icing and modelling chocolate, can be found in the same section. This is also true of the basic tutorial section, which leads you through a comprehensive 'how to' guide for everything from lining a cake pan to levelling, filling, covering, rodding and stacking. I also offer some specific technical guidance on piping, from how to hold a piping bag to how to control pressure. Read the front section carefully before embarking on a specific design project, so that you are properly armed with the right information and skills for success.

choosing your cake

There is no longer such a thing as a typical wedding, so why should there be a typical cake? The wedding style should be carefully considered to ensure the cake supports it and makes the right impact. The season of the wedding date is also important for design. Feminine florals in pastel colours effortlessly match up with spring and summer weddings, whereas rich, opulent colours and accents of gold are stunning for autumn or winter nuptials. More formal weddings naturally suit clean lines and sophisticated styles, such as Art Nouveau or Antique Lace, whereas laid-back, casual garden weddings lend themselves beautifully to more convivial designs, such as Spring Flowers or Vintage Rose. The number of guests can also be an important criterion. An intimate wedding would be the perfect setting for miniature cakes, such as those in the Film Noir and Something Borrowed... designs, but would be painstaking to achieve for a guest list of 200.

Of course colour schemes, themes, time of year and personal style will be leading factors in deciding how the cake should look, but when it comes to making a wedding cake, choosing the right design isn't just a matter of flicking through pictures and choosing your favourite. There are some practicalities you will need to consider first.

A PERFECT FINISH

Most people tend to think that the simpler the design, the easier. This is certainly true if you are well practised in covering and stacking cakes, but for those with less experience, creating a

professional-looking smooth finish can be difficult to achieve. Cracks, fingernail marks and billowing bottoms are just a few of the common mistakes made by inexperienced bakers. Following my guide to covering cakes on pages 28–31 will stand you in good stead, but it might be prudent to be a little flexible with your final design. A thicker ribbon and a few extra flowers can hide all manner of sins. But please don't be too hard on yourself if you need to rely on a little extra camouflage, I promise you that nobody will notice and everyone will be utterly impressed by all that you have achieved.

NUMBER OF GUESTS

The number of guests will affect the size of the cake you need to make, as will the decision about whether to serve the cake as dessert or with coffee later in the evening. A coffee portion is traditionally 2.5 cm/1 inch squared and a dessert portion is three times that size – or more, if you ask the venue staff or designated cake cutter to be more generous. It's also important to consider whether the bride and groom want to go down the traditional route of saving the top tier for their first anniversary, the christening/naming ceremony of their first child or to send to guests who are unable to attend on the day. If they do choose to save the top tier (see page 10), aside from making sure the rest of the cake will be big enough to feed the whole party, it is usually best to stick with tradition again and opt for a fruitcake as it can be preserved for longer.

I have deliberately chosen to stick to three-tiered designs in this book because it is the largest number of tiers you can stack and deliver in one piece. Even those creative and brave enough to make a DIY wedding cake will, I'm sure, feel less enthused by the idea of assembling the cake on the morning of the wedding. You should be getting your glad rags on, not getting your hands sticky.

If the wedding party is so large that even the largest three tiered cake won't suffice, I suggest you opt to make extra cutting cakes. Cutting cakes are large extra cakes, iced, but not decorated, that are not set up for display, but instead are sent straight to the kitchen for cutting. This makes particularly good sense if the cake is being served as dessert, as the kitchen staff can get a head start in prepping for service and the cake can be displayed in the reception hall for longer before it needs to be taken away to be sliced. Just ensure that if the cakes are cut early, they are covered until just before serving, to avoid all your hard work from drying out.

Having said that, I'm not interested in quashing anyone's zeal or ambitions. If you want to take on the challenge of a larger number of tiers, by all means go for it. Choose a design that doesn't spill over the tier edges and follow the guide for rodding all but the top tier. But please do not attempt delivery of the cake already fully stacked, as the likelihood of it surviving the journey intact will be left entirely to chance. Instead, take a piping bag of royal icing and a palette knife with you to the venue and stack the cakes on site.

A Guide To Storing Your Top Tier

If the top tier is to be saved, it is best to opt for a traditional, boozy fruitcake, which can be kept for a couple of years and even up to five, if stored correctly. (You can keep other cakes for up to three months in the freezer, but the flavours may diminish.) Wrap the cake (board included) very tightly in several layers of cling film/plastic wrap, put it in a plastic freezer box and freeze until needed. When required, defrost the cake and carefully remove the icing and marzipan with a sharp knife. Feed the cake with a little alcohol (dark rum or brandy), let the cake absorb its drink and then re-ice it. You can eat the defrosted top tier with the original marzipan and icing, but new icing will freshen up the look of the cake.

FLAVOURS

This book suggests natural pairings suitable for specific wedding styles and seasons. Although the flavour matches proffered are well thought out and sympathetic to each design, they are suggestions only and should not be seen as rigid or dictatorial. In terms of flavour, you must follow your own taste, and that may involve more than one. Most couples I work with are keen to offer their guests a choice, but if you do opt for a different flavour for every tier, it's important to think about how many people each tier will serve.

If you want an equal number of servings of each flavour, it is best to stick with two cake flavour options. If the top and middle tiers are one flavour and the base another, this will equate to roughly half and half in terms of the number of portions. This is a particularly sociable option if you are serving your cake as dessert, as guests tend to cut their slices in half and swap one half for half of another guest's alternative flavour.

You can also opt for a nod to tradition by choosing a fruitcake top tier. Another sensible option for the smallest tier is to choose a cake recipe that will cater for any guests with special dietary requirements, such as gluten, dairy or nut allergies. Alternatively, you can create an ultra special and indulgent flavour to be served exclusively to the top table, while keeping costs down with the type of cake chosen for the rest of your guests – just don't be surprised if a few envious glances are flashed in the top table's direction.

THE CUTTING OF THE CAKE

Don't forget to consider whether the cutting of the cake is an important moment to the bride and groom. It is a classic photo opportunity that most couples have included in their wedding albums. Traditionally, the couple hold the knife together and make the first cut in the base tier of their cake.

Cupcakes and miniature cakes are wonderful in that the portioning has already been done, so the cakes can be displayed until just moments before they are served. But, if you do opt for cupcakes or miniatures, the cutting of the cake moment will change. Some couples, for this reason, opt to have a top tier above their miniature cakes so that they have something to cut, such as in the Something Borrowed... design on page 91. Others simply feed each other a bite of cake as a modern twist on tradition.

YOU

Aside from these considerations, it is incredibly important to think seriously about the way you are likely to approach this task. Timing is everything here – when you will bake your cakes and when you will decorate them will inform what the best style of design is for you to work towards.

Do you like to have things done and dusted, with reams of time to spare? Or is it more likely that you'll be panicking two days before the wedding because you can't find that pan you could have sworn was at the back of the cupboard? Perhaps you're somewhere in between: you don't get stressed unduly, but aren't comfortable leaving anything to chance either. It's important to be honest with yourself before you begin, because the way you work as an individual should be a consideration for the kind of wedding cake you make.

Pre-planner

Are you the kind of person who would be in a blind panic if you had anything to complete at the last minute? Do you write endless 'to do' lists, which must be ticked off well in advance to avoid sleepless nights and nervous twitches? Does the idea of decorating the cake the day before the wedding day give you heart palpitations?

It's a wonderful trait to be organized and there are great things to be said for making sure everything is prepared in advance; that you know what you're doing and when and, most importantly, that you have the self-discipline to stick to your timetable. Despite all your admirable administrative skills, the average cake has a short life span, especially if, as well it should be, maintaining quality and freshness is of optimum importance to you. A traditional, boozy fruitcake will be the least stressful option for you, as a decent maturation time will always make the end results so much more temptingly delicious. But, we all know that what is best for our timetables might not be what's best for our taste buds and no one should have to compromise on flavour on their wedding day.

Personally, I adore fruitcake with all its sense of occasion and spicy warmth, but I know only too well that not everyone shares my enthusiasm for brandy-soaked raisins and currants. I feel sure my fruitcake recipe is good enough and boozy enough to convert the majority of you, but for the incurably fruitcake-phobic, there's absolutely no reason why you can't have a sponge or chocolate torte instead, as long as you're realistic with your design. I'd recommend choosing sugar or modelling chocolate decorations that can be made in advance and simply stuck on to your cake once it has been iced, so you have less to worry about in the days leading up to the big day. If you want to avoid high blood pressure, steer clear of any intricate hand piping or painting, which can only begin after the cakes have been iced. The same is true of chocolate ruffles; they can only be made once the cake is covered and ready to be dressed.

Last Minute

Are you the sort of person who, if you were given a hundred years to do something, would still need an extra day? Do you always seem to end up having to cram four hours' work into two, because, despite the best of intentions, you can't help but leave everything until the last possible moment? Just because you need the pressure of an imminent deadline to force you into action, you needn't feel that this task is out of your reach.

With the exception of fruitcake, the general rule of thumb is that the later you bake your cakes, the fresher they'll be and, as a result, the more moist and delicious. You see, being last minute isn't all bad; in fact, it can be a genuine bonus in cake baking.

Having said that, you'll want to be bright eyed and bushy tailed on the day itself, so leaving things so late that you are still wearing an apron with icing in your hair at 3 am on the morning of the wedding is a fate to be avoided at all costs. Don't spoil the day by being too ambitious with what you can achieve in the time you've got left.

It's best to stick to designs that don't require lots of sugar or chocolate work, which takes time to make and then needs time to set. Hand piping and painting will be your saving grace, as it's possible to create impressive designs and cover a lot of icing surface very quickly. Cupcakes are a great option as they bake and cool quickly and can be made and iced the day before. If you've run out of time to make the roses on the cupcakes (see page 96), there's no need to beat yourself up. A simple fondant punch-stamped heart or a scattering of pearly sugar balls are sure to go down a storm.

Don't be afraid to go for chocolate. As long as you avoid a style that requires you to make endless chocolate flowers in advance, you can get impressive results in no time. Why not cover your cakes in chocolate ganache for a beautiful, glossy finish that can be simply stacked and won't even need to be covered in marzipan first. Once the ganache has set, you can follow the step-by-step guidelines on page 82 for creating a stunning gold leaf effect or simply dress the cake with seasonal fruits or non-poisonous, unsprayed fresh flowers.

Little and Often

If you prefer to keep things balanced with a sense of easy-going order, you're unlikely to be overcome by the desire to get everything done a long time in advance, but nor will you appreciate the hassle of still having most of the work to do too close to the deadline. You probably think life is too short for the stress of boom and bust, and an all-or-nothing approach just isn't your style. Make life easy on yourself by choosing a design that can be achieved in fits and starts.

If you're already a keen baker, you'll know that chocolate cakes are all the better for being made a couple of days in advance, as their rich indulgence only improves after a spell in an airtight box, especially if coated in marzipan, ganache or modelling chocolate, as they all provide an airtight seal to lock in the moisture. You can make a chocolate cake on a Tuesday for a Saturday wedding, but you'd have to wait at least another 24 hours to start a vanilla sponge if you want it to be light and moist on the day.

You'll be more than able to cope with styles that require a combination of sugar work and piping. You can make your sugar flowers or butterflies at your own speed, in the weeks leading up to the wedding day, then the last-minute piping details won't phase you, as you can relax in the knowledge that a large proportion of the work has already been done.

Whatever your approach and whichever flavour and style you choose, don't forget to have a little fun. The designs in this book are only meant as guides. By all means, follow them exactly if you have fallen in love with one of the images presented, but please feel encouraged to use it as a launch pad for inspiration. The techniques shown in this book will help you develop the skills to enable you to run away with your imagination and create a bespoke design tailored to the special couple's unique style. You're the one making this wedding cake, so why not make it very much your own?

getting organized

If you haven't attempted baking or decorating on this sort of scale before, a trial run or two before the wedding day will certainly help to boost your confidence. If economy is your main objective, trial runs may well be an expense you can't afford. For a more cost-effective practice session for learning how to smoothly cover a cake, try downscaling the size. Once you master a 6-inch cake, a 12-inch won't be nearly as stressful when it comes to the real thing. As for piping practice, you won't need a cake at all, simply upturn a solid-bottomed cake pan and get to work with your piping bag. The icing will wash off easily and your practice dummy is ready for round two.

If you are already artistically persuaded, cocoa butter painting isn't much of a departure from watercolour painting in that you can build up layers of colour. But it has an attractive similarity with oil painting also as, once it has set, mistakes can be painted over. Cocoa butter has the added bonus that it takes minutes, rather than days, to dry.

Regardless of the wedding cake you choose, just a little bit of pre-planning is guaranteed to make your life so much simpler.

SOURCING YOUR EQUIPMENT

First things first, use the guide on page 140 to work out how big your cake will need to be to feed the number of guests attending. Once you know your cake sizes, you can source the right sized pans. The recipes in this book require a mixture of round, square, deep and shallow pans. (UK readers can use sandwich tins wherever recipes call for the use of two shallow cake pans.) There's no need to buy a brand new expensive pan that you're unlikely to use again. Many cake craft stockists hire out cake pans of all sizes at very reasonable prices (see page 158 for stockists).

The cake drum (the thick iced board your cake will be supported on will need to be at least 5–8 cm/2–3 inches larger in diameter than your base tier; so if your base cake is 30 cm/12 inches, you will need to buy a cake drum that is at least 35 cm/14 inches. It is the diameter of the cake drum, not the cake itself, that is the important figure if you decide to hire or buy a cake stand.

If the reception is at a venue regularly used for weddings, the venue will most likely already own a simple silver-plated round or square cake stand. If the wedding venue is as DIY as the cake, or if you have your sights set on something different, you will need to source a stand early on to avoid disappointment.

Don't forget to work out how you will be getting the cake to the venue. For detailed guidelines, see pages 14–15, but before you even get to that stage, you will need to buy a sturdy, purpose-made box. This is one thing you really don't want to have forgotten on the day.

Anything else you need will depend on the design you choose – be it new paintbrushes for cocoa butter designs, piping nozzles/tips,

cake rods or ribbons. If economy is your overriding motivation, it will be extremely worth your while to make a comprehensive list including absolutely everything you will need before you commit to buying a single thing. You may be surprised by what you are able to borrow from friends and family – from cake pans and measuring scales, to rolling pins and cake paddles.

DUTY OF CARE

However pretty your cake looks and however many different flavours you're offering the wedding guests, basic rules of food hygiene must be observed. If your oven is still harbouring last Christmas's goose fat splatters, it would be considerate to give it a thorough clean before any cake baking commences. If you can't quite face this daunting task, or if it has been so long that you'll need a chisel to cut through all the charred-on muck, don't despair. You can make an overdue appointment with a professional oven cleaning service who, at surprisingly little cost, come round and do it all for you.

It isn't only your oven that will need to be clean before you begin. If you have a pair of oven gloves hanging over the rail on your oven door that have been lingering longer than you'd care to admit, they will need to be laundered at a high temperature before they should be let anywhere near your cakes. Please remember that you are catering for tens and possibly hundreds of people, so you must take your duty of care seriously. If you are someone who is used to sticking your finger into the mixing bowl for a quick and guilty taste, you must be strict with yourself and resist the urge this time. It is a good idea to have a mugful of clean teaspoons on hand, to use for tasting as you go along. Just make sure there is no double dipping. Once a spoon has touched your lips, it must not find its way back into the buttercream.

Please do not be tempted to re-use cake boards. Once used, cake boards can contain bacteria even after careful washing. They must be thrown away or recycled to prevent your cakes from becoming mouldy and even potentially harmful to anyone eating off them.

Thorough and regular hand washing is essential, as is ensuring there is no cross-contamination with other foods prepared in the same kitchen. You shouldn't be making royal icing anywhere near a chopping board that has been used for meat or fish. It may sound obvious, but you will have to be extra rigorous – simply clean and clear as you go along and all should be fine. Think in terms of how you would want others to prepare food that you are going to eat, and if you are a little more relaxed than most in this area, simply close your eyes and call forth the spirit of your fussiest friend's wagging finger to keep your natural insouciance in check.

Fresh cream

Although I am actively encouraging you to get creative with your flavour choices, there is one alteration that should be avoided.

Freshly whipped cream, although delicious generously sandwiched between cakes, can become a microbiological hazard if left out of the fridge for more than four hours, or less time than that in hot weather. Fresh cream is not a practical filling for wedding cakes as they are, by their very nature, intended to be on display all day, and often in warm and badly ventilated marquees. You can always serve fresh cream on the side with your cake once it is cut as a compromise, or a wonderful alternative is vanilla-scented mascarpone, a decadently smooth and creamy filling, which is safe to leave out of the fridge for a much longer time.

Yes, be vigilant, but don't give yourself a nervous breakdown. These are all basic food hygiene rules that only look daunting because they are written down in black and white. You needn't get overly flustered by any of this, it's all just simple common sense. Just tie your hair back, put plasters on any cuts on your fingers, roll up your sleeves and get on with the task in hand.

Pets

I am a great animal lover, but not in the kitchen. If you are usually carefree about cats climbing over your worktops while you cook, I'm afraid, for this particular task, you will have to adopt a more diligent style. I'm not suggesting that your beloved pets should be banished from the house entirely, but it would be sagacious to keep the kitchen door closed and to vacuum up any pet hairs and disinfect the floor and worktops before you begin. After all, nobody wants to find a Labrador hair in their slice of Lemon drizzle.

WHAT TO WEAR

Some years ago, a friend of a friend emailed me for advice on how to make her sister's wedding cake. Her main concerns were focused on what she should wear. 'Do I need to buy special chefs' whites or will an apron be OK?' she asked, 'and I've already made a fruitcake tier, but I didn't wear a hairnet. Do you think I should throw it away and start again?' Although I applauded her cautiousness, if you become too overly anxious about everything, you will spend the wedding day dreading the moment the cake is cut, instead of glowing with pride at all you have achieved.

You do not need to wear chefs' whites, but I would definitely recommend wearing a clean apron, to protect your clothes, if nothing else. Whatever you decide to wear, make sure it is freshly laundered and preferably made of cotton or another material that does not shed. Avoid fluffy knits that could leave floating fibres in your chocolate ganache or royal icing. A plain white or cream top is my uniform of preference, especially when decorating. It is amazing how easily fibres from dark fabrics or denim can settle on your crisp white sugarpaste, only to become embedded inside after kneading. You can avoid wasting time picking out pesky, unsightly fibres with a scribe tool, by ensuring all your clothes are cake friendly to begin with.

It certainly wouldn't be bad practice to wear a hairnet or hat, but it really isn't a necessary requirement. As long as you tie your hair back so that it is off your face, and remove any jewellery before you begin, you are good to go.

getting it there

Getting your finished cake to the reception venue is, by far, the most nerve-wracking part of the whole process. Although you can never guarantee a cake's safe delivery (accidents do, after all, happen), there are precautions you can implement to reduce the risks to almost zero.

I'd highly recommend a test drive to the venue in the weeks ahead. Be sure to take note of any potholes, cattle grids, steep hills or sudden declines in the road and also check the entrance of the reception venue for speed bumps, which wedding venues seem to have a particular and irritating fondness for. It's often worth double-checking that there isn't an alternative speed bump-free entrance around the back. If the journey to the venue is uncompromisingly treacherous, you can do one of two things: either take the cake in single tiers in separate small boxes and assemble it onsite, or cross your fingers and hope for the best. It really depends how close to the edge you like to live.

You can buy large, deep boxes designed specifically for the transportation of stacked cakes (see page 158 for stockists). They come in a wide range of sizes and have a cut out square or round dip that your cake board should fit snuggly into to prevent your

cake from sliding during transit. Carefully lift the cake and position it in the cake board dip. You may feel safer asking someone else to hold the box securely while you do this. If yours is a particularly heavy cake, you may need to slide a step palette knife underneath the cake to prevent you from trapping your fingers.

The box should be lifted only at the base, with the weight of the cake supported on your forearms. Bear in mind that reception rooms are often at the other end of long corridors or even up or down flights of stairs, so if you don't have the physical strength to do this alone, you will need to travel with an accomplice to help you set the cake up in position.

Place a non-slip mat underneath the cake box to prevent it from sliding. It sounds obvious enough, but do check that your box will actually fit into your boot/trunk before you stagger over to the car on the morning of the wedding, straining beneath the weight of several kilos of cake, only to discover that there isn't a shoehorn in the world big enough to help you squeeze it in there.

A little 'Wedding Cake On Board' card, visibly placed in your rear window will help ensure fellow travellers on the road are more sympathetic to your slow driving and they will be less inclined to panic you by getting too close to your tail. Drive calmly and steadily and make sure you leave for the venue in good time.

A final note on the delivery vehicle... even if it is freezing outside, do not, under any circumstances, put the heater on. Buttercream and ganache may melt and your cake might collapse with any interior structural changes that such melting could cause. It is better that you suffer a little discomfort in the perishing cold for the sake of a safe journey, than for your cake to perish for the sake of a comfortable one. Equally, if you are making the delivery on a very hot day, crank up the air conditioning as high as you can bear and please refrain from packing the cake in the boot/trunk long before you are ready to leave for the venue. A stationary car on a hot day will always be hotter than when it's on the move, so desist from any urges to be too eager to get things done. In this instance, you'll be shooting yourself in your organized foot. What you can pack in advance is a bag containing all the things you will need for setting up your cake and a patch kit.

A patch kit should contain a step palette knife to help you lift the cake out of its box, as well as extra ribbon, fabric scissors and a non-toxic glue stick, just in case. If you are transporting the cake to a venue that may have an uneven floor, such as a marquee, it is wise to pack a few pieces of cardboard in case you need to fix a wobbly table leg. What you need for your patch kit will depend on the design you choose. A few extra sugar/chocolate decorations, in case anything has fallen off during transit, is a good idea and you will also need piping bags fitted with the appropriate nozzles/tips and filled with the appropriately coloured royal icing for patching up any chipped or shattered piping details. You probably won't need to open your patch kit at all, but it's always best to err on the side of caution and it's hugely comforting on the journey there to know you have it with you.

PRESENTING YOUR CAKE

Since there's barely a wedding album in existence that doesn't include at least one snap of this iconic cake, you'll be well served to pick a spot where it is easily visible to everyone and which also has a decent background to set the scene nicely. You don't want to head back down nostalgia's highway ten years down the line, to see pictures of your beautiful cake being upstaged by an emergency exit sign or an ugly radiator with peeling paint. The same can be said of an un-ironed tablecloth. If the venue has a table beautiful enough not to need a tablecloth, you'll be extremely fortunate. For the most part, a tablecloth is an essential extra and also hides any gifts for the bridesmaids until they are given out during the speeches. Aside from ensuring your tablecloth is crease-free, it is advisable to pick a fabric sympathetic to the cake's design. The right choice of tablecloth can do wonders for highlighting the cake, so think about colours, textures and formality.

Although you don't need to present the cake on a cake stand, if you do choose to do so, you will need to consider the style carefully. Cake stands create extra height, which aid visibility and add an extra sense of occasion. Options range massively from silver or gold plated and clear or coloured glass, either plain or etched, to china stands in a rainbow of colours and with hugely differing levels of detail. If you are presenting towers of cupcakes or miniatures, you may find that your only real option is to source a special cupcake stand from a cake craft supplier.

Special cake knives and swords can be bought or hired from most cake craft suppliers, but if you are hoping for something more individual or antique in style, but haven't been the fortunate recipient of a passed-down family heirloom, boot fairs and antique markets can offer a wealth of choice. If the knife is bought especially for the wedding, it is a lovely touch to consider getting it engraved with the bride and groom's names and the wedding date.

Once the table has been positioned and checked for stability and your chosen tablecloth has been pressed, place your chosen cake stand (if using) in the correct position. If you are presenting the cake on a separate cake table, as is the norm, the cake generally looks best positioned in the centre of the table. This should give you ample room for dressing the table with any extras, such as petals, floral displays, sugared almonds or candles.

If the wedding cake is to be presented in the middle of a room, so that the guests can walk all the way around the cake, it will need to be presentable from every angle. A good trick is to work it so that the designs spills over the ribbon joins – a single blossom attached to the ribbon can hide a join or cascading flowers can happily sweep over and cover them up.

You want to make the cake the centre of attention in the reception room, but not because it slid off an uneven table during the speeches. Make sure your cake is well supported. The key things to remember when presenting the cake are stability, visibility and atmosphere. If you are mindful of these three things, all should be fine.

why things go wrong...

Sometimes, even for the most experienced bakers, things go wrong. Don't panic, it doesn't mean they'll always go wrong. Please don't let it put you off reaching for your apron altogether – it doesn't mean you can't bake just because your cake sank in the middle that one time. Don't let a few baking mishaps push you into the chemically-enhanced grasp of supermarket cakes – just roll up your sleeves and try again. I've put together a list in the hope that if you understand why things might have gone wrong in the first place, it will hopefully be easier to avoid more baking disasters in the future. But first: ovens.

It's essential that you know your oven. For fan ovens, always remember to reduce the temperature slightly. Some ovens are like kilns and others seem to be much hotter on one side than the other. If you know what your oven is like, you can adjust temperatures and rituals accordingly. Reduce the temperature by 20 degrees or so for a very hot oven or turn the cake round halfway through cooking for ovens with hot spots. And lastly, it really is important to always preheat your oven to the required temperature before popping your cake in. So here goes the list, I hope it helps...

A burnt top and a wobbly middle: This is usually due to your oven being too hot, but it can also be due to your mixture being too slack. For very damp cakes, such as cakes that include fresh fruit (apples, plums, etc.), the cooking times often need to be increased and the temperature of your oven reduced. A very wet batter can lead to the top cooking before the middle has caught up. The way to combat this is usually as simple as placing a piece of baking parchment or foil over the top of the cake for the second half of the cooking time.

A sunken middle: This can be caused by a few different factors. Too much baking powder, under-cooking or over-beating (causing over-aeration) can all cause sinking, but more often it is caused by opening the oven door too quickly. Try to avoid opening the oven door before 15 minutes is up, so that the oven temperature can remain stable and your cake, in turn, can hopefully remain stable too. Altitude can also affect how a cake rises, so if you live over 2,500 feet above sea level, you may have to adjust your oven temperature and cooking time and reduce the quantity of raising agent. When egg whites are the sole raising agent in a cake, whisk them only to the soft peak stage to prevent your cakes from deflating.

A peak and a crack: Sometimes cakes peak on top and then crack, this is usually due to the temperature of your oven being too hot or (for non fan-assisted ovens) the cake being placed too high up. If your cake is placed on too high a shelf, it forms a crust too quickly; the raising agents continue working so the cake continues to rise and cracks its crusted top. Try reducing the temperature by 20 degrees and always place your cakes on the middle shelf, or lower for particularly large or tall cakes.

Bready cake: We all want our sponge cakes to be light and fluffy, but everyone has tasted a sponge that is heavy enough to do some damage with if used as a missile in the direction of someone's head. This is due to overbeating the mixture, which overworks the gluten in the flour and gives the cake a bready texture. I know it can be

dull, especially when a recipe calls for a large amount of flour or cocoa, but it really is worth sifting, so you won't have to beat the mixture to within an inch of its life just to get the lumps out. It's also worth checking the 'use by' dates on self-raising flour and raising agents. People often have bags of flour at the back of the cupboard that are months or even years out of date. Checking the date becomes particularly tricky for those who like to decant their flours into other containers, so it's worth making the effort to attach a label with their 'best before' dates. Raising agents stop working after a while and out-of-date self-raising flour becomes inactive. All flours can become stale and are very susceptible to picking up odours from other foods, so never keep your flour in the same place as anything with a pong – onions, garlic, chilli, herbs, spices, etc. Another rather nasty potential hazard for old flour is weevils, which you will certainly want to avoid!

It won't rise: When cakes don't rise it is because: insufficient or no raising agents have been added; the flour or raising agents used are too old and therefore inactive (see above); the mixture is too stiff (you can slacken the mixture by adding a drop of milk), or overbeaten so that all the air has been knocked out. The temperature of your oven may play a part here, too, as cakes won't rise if your oven is too cool.

A dry cake: I have a massive aversion to dry cakes. The pleasure of cake eating is lost to me when it is too dry and although icing can do something to mask the insult, it will still feel like a disappointing waste of calories. Dry cakes can be blamed on too much baking powder, overcooking or when the cooled cake is not packed immediately or is stored in a container which is not properly airtight.

Runny whites: Egg whites are funny old things. If you whisk them into stiff peaks and then carry on whisking for long enough afterwards, they turn back into liquid. If you whisk them and leave them lying about for too long before using them, they also become runny again. In both cases you will never be able to whisk them back into peaks. If egg whites get even the tiniest trace of fat in them, they will never fluff up, however long you whisk them for. This is why you must avoid getting any yolk in with the whites. Egg yolks are the fat of the egg, and the whites are the protein. Their fat content is the reason why, until fairly recently, people thought eggs were bad for you, due to their cholesterol and fat content. Since we now know these fats are essential healthy fats, we can throw caution to the wind and eat them with gluttonous abandon. To avoid getting fat in your whites, make sure the bowl you use is completely clean and oil free. You can even wipe half a lemon around the inside of the bowl first to remove any traces of oil as an extra precaution. You must also make sure you are very careful not to get any traces of yolk in with the whites while you are separating them. I find, when separating a large number of eggs, a sensible precaution is

to separate each egg, one at a time, over a small bowl, before adding them to your big bowl of whites. You don't want to have separated 29 out of 30 eggs, only to break the yolk of the 30th into all those whites. What a tragic waste of all that time and all those eggs that would be. Another good tip is to add a pinch of salt to the whites before whisking, as it becomes almost impossible to overbeat them. I can't pretend to understand the reason for this, but all I know is that it works and that's good enough for me.

Now that you know how to avoid potential pitfalls, you are on course for making some truly delicious cakes. Good luck!

essential recipes and techniques

Whatever cake flavour or design you choose, there are a number of techniques and recipes that will keep coming up again and again. Where instructed, turn to this section for basic recipes and clear directions for essential cake decorating techniques.

1. Electric mixer
2. Folding flower stand
3. Turntable
4. Cake pans
5. Weighing scales
6. Chocolate scraper
7. Various sized cake boards and cake drums
8. Paintbrushes
9. Large silicone rolling pin
10. Ruler
11. Small silicone rolling pin
12. Cake tester
13. Edible ink pens
14. Modelling tools
15. Piping nozzles/tips
16. Metal cutters
17. Plastic plunge cutters
18. Metal plunge cutters
19. Daisy centre moulds
20. Plastic cutters
21. Rejuvenator fluid
22. Cake paddles
23. Various sieves/strainers
24. Foam flower shaper
25. Foam modelling mat
26. Dowelling rods
27. Palette knives
28. Small, sharp knife
29. Rubber spatulas
30. Pastry brush

essential recipes

Some recipes are at the heart of whatever cake you are creating. This section is a reference point to return to for essential recipes such as royal icing, marzipan and modelling chocolate. All of these can be bought ready-prepared, but can be cheaper and taste so much better if you prepare them yourself. Don't be daunted if you haven't made anything similar before – these recipes are very simple to follow.

royal icing

Royal icing is a fantastic tool for any cake maker. It works as an essential glue for stacking cakes and attaching sugar and chocolate pieces, as well as being the key ingredient for creating beautiful piped designs. Royal icing can also be used as a covering. It creates sharper lines than sugar paste and must be built up in several layers using a palette knife. When piping, it is always best to use royal icing on the day it has been made, but it can be stored in an airtight container for up to a week, with a sheet of damp kitchen paper placed over the top of the icing before the lid is sealed. The egg white separates if left for longer than a day, so the royal icing will need to be whisked again before it can be used. If the use of raw egg white concerns you, you can replace it with powdered egg white, following the manufacturer's instructions for quantities.

1 large egg white
325 g/2⅓ cups icing/
confectioners' sugar
freshly squeezed juice
of ½–1 lemon

Put the egg white in a large mixing bowl and remove any stringy white pieces (chalazae) that may clog your piping nozzle/tip later.

Sift over half of the icing/confectioners' sugar and whisk with an electric hand whisk on a low speed until the sugar is fully incorporated. Sift over the remaining icing/confectioners' sugar and whisk again. The mixture will start to resemble breadcrumbs.

Add the juice of ½ a lemon and whisk until the mixture turns into a thick paste. Keep whisking on high speed for a couple of minutes. You may need to add a little more lemon juice at this stage, depending on the desired thickness. You should be left with a beautifully glossy icing, which is stiff enough to use for piping, but soft enough so that your piped lines will not break.

marzipan

Marzipan makes a brilliant undercoat. Icing a tiered cake with marzipan before sugar paste ensures a much more structurally stable result, especially if you have opted for particularly gooey tortes or gluten-free cakes. A marzipan undercoat also provides a more seamless and professional finish, as well as helping to lock in a cake's moisture. If you can't stand the stuff, you can use two layers of sugar paste instead, as long as you let the first coat crust properly before adding a second. A better alternative is to cover the cakes in modelling chocolate – either instead of sugar paste altogether or, if rolled more thinly, as a base layer for your icing.

Marzipan tends to divide opinion strongly. Some view it as the confectionery equivalent of a romantic weekend away in Paris, believing its inclusion leads only to ever more delicious possibilities. Others turn their noses up at our almond-flavoured friend, lamenting its sorry inclusion in their favourite sweet treats and regarding it as an unwelcome gate crasher at an otherwise enjoyable party. If you fall into the latter camp, let me reassure you that home-made marzipan is nothing like the lurid yellow abomination masquerading as marzipan in the aisles of some supermarkets. If you like almonds, but abhor marzipan, it's probably the taste of fake almond essence you struggle with and not the marzipan itself. You may want to reconsider your stance and try giving it another go, or personalize the recipe by adding the scraped out seeds of a vanilla pod or perhaps the zest of a lemon. For a twist on tradition, you can replace the ground almonds with ground pistachios or hazelnuts. You can try adding orange zest and a splash of Cointreau for extra lift, or, if you're feeling adventurous, you can substitute a fifth of the icing/confectioners' sugar for cocoa to make chocolate marzipan.

Using the recipes below as a basis, you can add your own unique flavour stamp – a few drops of rose water or lavender extract or a dusting of cinnamon or ground ginger are just a few of the possibilities. Have fun playing with your flavours, just don't add too much liquid or your marzipan will become too sticky to work with. If this all sounds too much like hard work, there are some excellent ready-made marzipans available these days – just opt for the 'natural' varieties if you want to avoid the disgusting lurid yellow kind.

simple marzipan

This method is incredibly quick and easy and gives stable results. It is the kind of marzipan that used to be known as 'almond paste' and is probably what your mother uses to cover her Christmas cake. I never add almond extract, but if you like the taste of nostalgia it brings, by all means add a drop or two if you wish.

250 g/1¾ cups icing/confectioners' sugar, sifted

250 g/1¼ cups (caster) sugar

500 g/1 lb. 2 oz. (5 cups) ground almonds

4 large egg whites, lightly beaten

freshly squeezed juice of ½ lemon

1 tablespoon brandy

Makes 1 kg/2¼ lbs.

Put the sugars and ground almonds in a large mixing bowl and stir together. Create a well in the middle and add the eggs, lemon juice and brandy. Use a fork to start incorporating the wet and dry ingredients. When everything is roughly mixed, discard the fork and use your hands to knead the mixture together until you have a firm, stiff ball of dough. Don't overwork the dough, though, or your marzipan will become greasy. Wrap the ball of dough in cling film/plastic wrap and leave in a cool place until ready to use.

rich marzipan

Although slightly more complicated to make, the texture of this marzipan is less rustic and more silky and luxurious. Rich marzipan can be a little stickier to work with, so you may need some extra icing/confectioners' sugar on hand just in case. The eggs in this version are cooked through, so this is a better choice if raw eggs are a concern to you.

2 large eggs, plus 1 egg yolk

500 g/3⅔ cups icing/confectioners' sugar

2 teaspoons lemon juice

2 tablespoons brandy

500 g/1 lb. 2 oz. (5 cups) ground almonds

Makes 1 kg/2¼ lbs.

Put the eggs, egg yolk and sugar in a large heatproof bowl set over a pan of barely simmering water. Whisk continuously with a balloon or electric whisk until the mixture is pale, thick and doubled in volume. Make sure you keep the heat low or the mixture will get too hot and curdle. Whisk in the lemon juice and brandy until thoroughly combined, then take the bowl off the heat and leave to cool. When cool, whisk again, pour in the ground almonds and stir to combine thoroughly, then knead to form a firm dough. Wrap the marzipan in cling film/plastic wrap and leave to rest somewhere cool for at least 2 hours before rolling out.

modelling chocolate

Modelling chocolate is a versatile beast. I often liken it to chocolate plasticine, as it is so adaptable and can be sculpted into almost anything. It makes beautiful chocolate flowers, leaves and shapes and is the perfect cake covering for those who want softer edges than chocolate ganache gives, without losing the chocolatey flavour. When used as a cake covering, modelling chocolate can be used on its own or kneaded, half and half with sugarpaste. It can be rather stiff to work with, especially in cold weather, so does require more kneading than sugarpaste, but blasting it in the microwave for ten-second intervals can help to make it more malleable. If you get carried away and zap it for too long, just pop it in the fridge for ten minutes to firm up. Modelling chocolate can, especially in hot weather and especially the white chocolate variety, become sticky and even greasy when over-handled – this usually only happens when making intricate decorations, rather than when just rolling it out. Just keep regularly washing your hands in cold water and try to work on a cool surface (marble is ideal) to combat this should the issue arise. Finally, when using white modelling chocolate as a cake covering, use icing/confectioners' sugar to stop it sticking, just as you would with sugarpaste. For dark modelling chocolate use cocoa powder and for milk chocolate use a mixture of cocoa powder and icing/confectioners' sugar.

TEMPERING CHOCOLATE

There are a lot of things in life to be frightened of, but tempering chocolate shouldn't be one of them. Tempering is simply a heating and cooling process at controlled temperatures to ensure the crystals in the chocolate remain as small and stable as possible, so that the chocolate will have a lovely 'snap', retain its gloss and be deliciously smooth when it melts on your tongue. Tempering is essential to prevent your chocolate from 'blooming' – the white, matte streaks sometimes seen on chocolate. This is especially important when decorating, as poor tempering will result in a poor finish. The easiest method, aside from buying a tempering machine, is the seeding method. You will need a chocolate thermometer to ensure complete accuracy, which can be sourced very inexpensively. As well as using tempered chocolate for making modelling chocolate, you can make all manner of decorations, pipe with it or dip truffles and/or fruits in it. If you would like coloured chocolate, you can also buy specialist cocoa butter dyes to add when tempering – just follow the manufacturer's instructions for use.

1 Finely chop your chocolate (you can give it a quick blitz in a food processor if you're short on time), place two thirds in a heatproof bowl set over a pan of barely simmering water and melt gently. You can give it a stir with a rubber spatula every now and then to help move things along. Make sure the bottom of the bowl doesn't touch the water or your chocolate may seize.

2 Once the chocolate has melted, take the bowl off the heat and add the remaining chopped chocolate. Pop your thermometer into the chocolate and stir continuously until it reaches 31–32°C/88–90°F for dark chocolate, 29–30°C/84–86°F for milk chocolate, or 28–29°C/82–84°F for white chocolate. Your chocolate is now tempered and ready for use.

PREPARING MODELLING CHOCOLATE

You must prepare the modelling chocolate at least one day before use, but it keeps for up to two months wrapped tightly in clingfilm/plastic wrap and sealed in an airtight container. Ensure that the modelling chocolate is stored somewhere cool and dry. Modelling chocolate, particularly dark, can be hard work to knead. You can soften it in the microwave, or, if you don't have one, you can cut it into small pieces. The heat of your hands will soften it more quickly if you work with it in small amounts at a time.

dark modelling chocolate

400 g/14 oz. liquid glucose
500 g/1 lb. 2 oz. dark chocolate
(60% cocoa solids), tempered

Makes 900 g/2 lbs.

Warm the liquid glucose gently in a saucepan. When it reaches 40°C (104°F), pour it into the tempered dark chocolate. Vigorously stir the mixture with a wooden spoon until it is completely smooth. This needs a bit of elbow grease, so be patient. Once ready, pour the modelling chocolate into a large, clean (and preferably zip-locked) plastic food bag and leave at room temperature for at least one day to set. Once set, the modelling chocolate is ready to use.

white modelling chocolate

400 g/14 oz. liquid glucose
650 g/1 lb. 7 oz. white chocolate, tempered

Makes just over 1 kg/2¼ lbs.

Warm the liquid glucose gently in a saucepan. When it reaches 40°C (104°F), pour it into the tempered white chocolate. Vigorously stir the mixture with a wooden spoon until it is completely smooth. This needs a bit of elbow grease, so be patient. Once ready, pour the modelling chocolate into a large, clean (and preferably zip-locked) plastic food bag and leave at room temperature for at least one day to set. Once set, the modelling chocolate is ready to use.

tip: buying dark chocolate to model

When buying dark chocolate to temper for modelling chocolate, don't pick one that has more than 60% cocoa solids, or your modelling chocolate won't be malleable enough to work with.

essential techniques

This chapter takes you through the basics, from lining a cake pan and covering a cake in marzipan and sugar paste, to how to rod and stack your cake tiers ready for decorating and making paper piping bags. You can keep coming back to this chapter for useful piping tips and techniques and once you've mastered these key basics, you will be armed with the right tools to go on to more intricate design work and will have gained the confidence to realize your own creative ideas.

lining cake pans

It is a dull but necessary stage to baking that you must grease and line your pans, but if you follow the steps below, you will find it quick and trouble free. It is important when lining pans that you ensure that the baking parchment fits snugly and is wrinkle free – this will result in a good shaped cake without indentations. It is not necessary to line the edges of shallow cake pans (sandwich tins) with baking parchment. Just place a disc or square in the bottom of the pan and liberally grease the sides with butter before pouring in your cake batter.

1 Cut a square piece of baking parchment, slightly bigger than your cake pan. Place the sheet inside the pan and push it firmly into the corners or around the edges of the pan with your fingers to create a crease around the diameter of the base. **(A)**

2 Remove the parchment and use clean paper scissors to cut around the creased line so you have a circle or square

of parchment that fits the base of your pan perfectly. **(B)**

3 Next, cut long strips of baking parchment a little wider than the height of your pan, so they will protrude above the top.

4 Grease the inside of your pan with butter or oil and line the base of the pan with your cut-out circle or square. **(C)**

5 Wrap the long strips around the inside edge of the pan **(D)** – they should stick to the greased sides. If your strips aren't long enough, you can always cut an extra piece to cover any exposed sides.

tip: preparing pans for fruit cakes

As baking times are longer for fruit cakes, it is best to double-line your pans, as well as tie a double layer of brown parcel paper around the outside of the pan with string. This will help protect the cake and prevent the base and outside edges from burning.

A

B

C

D

A

B

C

D

how to level a cake

If your cake has a less than perfect bake, or if you didn't level the cake batter evenly enough before it went in the oven, fear not. A peaked top can be trimmed off with little effort. To avoid unnecessary cake waste or being left with a shallow overall result, follow the trouble-shooting guide on pages 16–17 in the hope that you can skip this section altogether. But don't be too hard on yourself if your cake doesn't exit the oven perfectly even – it won't stop it being every bit as tasty. Do wait until all your tiers have been baked before you take a knife to any of them though, as it is important to assess them in relation to each other. Measure them all with a ruler – any differences in height greater than 5 mm/¼ inch may mean some of your cakes require a quick trim.

1 First, measure the depth of all the cakes with a ruler, measuring all the way around the circumference to find the most shallow section. Use this height as the measure for all of your cake heights.

2 In turn, move the ruler around the sides of each cake, making small incisions to mark the right height.

3 Using a long, serrated knife, cut into the first incision and, turning the cake as you carve all the way around, make sure your cutting remains level with the incisions you made earlier. **(A)**

4 Once you have gone all the way around the cake, carefully lift the carved top off the cake. Repeat these steps for any of your other cakes which need levelling.

how to slice a cake

Before measuring up your cake to be sliced, level the top first to ensure you find its true centre point. I have suggested slicing your cakes horizontally into only two layers, but if you would prefer your cakes to have three, or even four layers, by all means go for it. You will need to up the quantity of buttercream and please bear in mind that the more layers you create, the trickier it will be to cover in marzipan, modelling chocolate or sugar paste later on. I'd recommend taking the time to practise with a small cake first, ahead of time.

1 Use a ruler to mark the central point of the cake and make a few small incisions around the sides at this point. **(B)**

2 Using a long, serrated knife, carve the cake horizontally, turning the cake as you cut, until you have cut all the way through. **(C)**

3 Carefully lift one half off and the cake is now ready to be spread with your chosen filling. **(D)**

tip: for an easier slice

Some cakes, particularly gluten-free cakes, can be more difficult to level and slice in half. If your chosen cake is particularly close-textured and fudgy, your knife will become loaded with claggy cake crumbs as you work. Dunking your knife in boiling water before wiping it dry, can help it to glide through the cake more easily when you start cutting.

A | B | C | D

dyeing sugar paste

Always use a food colouring paste to tint sugar paste, floristry paste and marzipan as liquid dye will make them too sticky to work with. Paste dyes are very concentrated, so it is easy to over-colour icing if you add too much too quickly, so be frugal at first – you can always add more if you need to, but once it's been added, you can't take it away. A word of warning, always wear latex gloves when kneading in the colour if you don't want to dye your hands, too!

1 Knead the sugar paste until it is pliable **(A)**, then add a small amount of dye with a cocktail stick/toothpick. **(B)** (If you are dying larger amounts, or for bolder colours, you can add the colouring paste with a butter knife.)

2 Knead the colour into the sugar paste **(C)**, adding a little more paste and kneading again if you need a stronger colour. This can take quite a while, so be patient as you'll want it to be streak-free when it's on your cake.

3 Once dyed **(D)**, wrap your icing in a clean plastic bag, expel the air and tie it up, to stop it drying out. Leave it to rest for 15 minutes before rolling it out. Resting it helps to prevent air bubbles forming.

covering a cake drum

Covering the cake drum with icing creates a professional and clean finish. You can match the colour of the sugar paste on your cake to your cake drum or use a complementary shade from elsewhere in the cake design for a bolder end result.

1 Knead your sugar paste until soft and pliable, then mould it into the right shape – a ball for a round cake and a cube for a square. Roll out the sugar paste on a surface lightly dusted with icing/confectioners' sugar, and smooth over it with a paddle to make sure there are no lumps or bubbles. **(A)**

2 Working quickly so your paste won't dry out, brush the cake drum with a 40% proof spirit or, for the teetotal amongst you, cooled boiled water will work just as well. Lift the sugar paste by draping it over your rolling pin and lay it over the cake drum. **(B)**

3 Smooth over the cake drum with a cake paddle until you have a perfectly smooth and polished top. **(C)**

4 Place the cake drum on a turntable and use a small, sharp knife to trim away the excess sugar paste. **(D)** Leave the iced board to dry overnight or for at least 8 hours. You can even complete this stage a few weeks before if you like.

A | B | C | D

A

B

C

D

preparing a cake for icing

The technique for filling and covering is largely the same whether you have split a single cake, or baked two shallow cakes. The only minor difference is that split cakes will shed extra crumbs. You can, if you wish, crumb coat your cakes by following steps 1 and 2, before covering the top and sides with a small scraping of buttercream – just enough to seal in the crumbs. Transfer the crumb-coated cake to the fridge to firm up for 15 minutes before continuing with step 3.

1 Attach one half of cake to a thin cake board of the same size with a small blob of buttercream. **(A)**

2 Spread the top of the first cake with half of the buttercream/filling with a palette knife **(B)** before sandwiching the second cake on top. Make sure you have positioned the cakes so the sides are straight – you don't want to have to correct a wonky cake at a later stage.

3 Transfer the cake to a turntable and spread the remaining buttercream/filling over the top of the cake ensuring you create a really smooth even surface. **(C)**

4 Cover the sides of the cake by positioning the flat edge of a palette knife, slightly at an angle, onto the side of the cake and turn the turntable as you smooth the buttercream neatly around the edges of the cake. **(D)** Scrape any excess off your palette knife every now and then.

5 Once you have the desired even, straight-edged finish, pop the cake in the fridge for about 20 minutes for the buttercream to set.

If you are covering a fruit cake in marzipan, it is best to omit the buttercream. Instead, follow the instructions below for coating the cake in jam so that the marzipan will adhere to the cake.

1 Put a few tablespoons of apricot (or other flavour-appropriate) jam into a saucepan and heat until it becomes runny, then press it through a sieve/strainer to remove any lumps.

2 Brush the cake board with the warmed jam **(A)** and place the cake on top. **(B)**

3 Brush the top and sides of the cake with the remaining jam and proceed directly to the covering instructions overleaf.

A

B

C

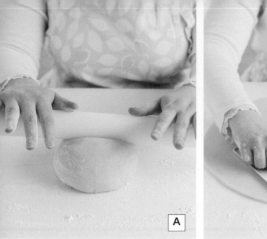

covering a cake with marzipan

For multi-layered cakes, it is always best to cover your cakes with marzipan before sugarpaste, to create extra stability and a clean and flawless finish. This is especially true if you are making a gooey dessert cake or a gluten-free cake, as they tend to be more crumbly and soft textured. If you aren't a fan of marzipan or are catering for guests with nut allergies, you can replace the marzipan with an extra layer of sugar paste or a thin layer of modelling chocolate before icing. Whichever type of cake you are covering, each individual tier should have been placed on a thin cake board, the same size as the cake, and the surface prepared with buttercream, jam or similar (see page 27). If you have left your buttercream or ganache-covered cake to set for so long that its surface has hardened too much for the marzipan to stick to it, quickly brush the top and sides with brandy (or a flavour-sensitive alcohol) or cooled boiled water using a pastry brush.

1 Knead your marzipan until it is soft and pliable and mould it into the correct shape for the cake you are covering before you start to roll it out – a ball for a round cake and a cube for a square cake.

2 Dust the work surface with icing/confectioners' sugar and roll out the marzipan to a thickness of around 5 mm/¼ inch. **(A)** There is no need to turn the marzipan over – only roll one side. If it begins to stick, simply dust underneath the marzipan sheet with more icing/confectioners' sugar.

3 Check your rolled sheet of marzipan is big enough by using a piece of string to measure your cake, making sure you include the sides in the calculation. When the marzipan is the right size, smooth over the surface with a cake paddle to smooth out any unevenness. **(B)**

4 Lift the marzipan off the surface with the rolling pin, and gently roll it off the pin onto your cake. **(C)**

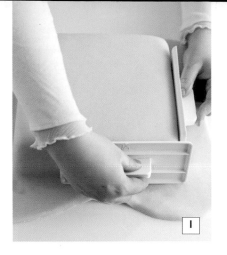

tip: covering square cakes

When covering square cakes with marzipan or icing, the process is largely the same as that in the main method, but be aware of the sides and edges. Once you have carefully rolled the marzipan onto your cake, firmly pat the top of the cake to ensure the marzipan has properly adhered. Cup your hands around the edges and sides of the cake, then pat the sides with flat hands and smooth the edges to a soft point. Trim off most of the excess marzipan and use cake paddles to firmly smooth the sides, sliding them to meet at each angle to emphasize the edges. **(I)** Smooth over the top in the same way, making sure all edges are kept fairly sharp. Lift your cake onto a turntable or upturned bowl and use the paddles again to really ensure the sides of the cake are straight.

5 Using your hands, quickly smooth over the top of the cake and then, with a cupping motion, pat down the sides of the cake, ensuring all the marzipan has been fully stuck down and all air has been expelled. **(D)** If you find you have trapped a large pocket of air, gently lift the marzipan off the cake and place it back down using the other hand to expel the air pocket as you do so. If you find any air bubbles, use a scribe tool or sterilized needle to prick the bubble at a 90° angle, before gently stroking the air out of the hole with your other hand. Once the air bubble has been expelled, use your cake paddles to smooth over the area.

6 Using cake paddles, smooth over the top of the cake in a circular motion, then work around the sides of your cake in forward circular motions. **(E)**

7 Trim off most of the excess marzipan with a small, sharp knife **(F)**, then lift the cake onto a turntable and use the paddles to go around the sides of the cake once more to make sure you have a perfectly smooth finish. **(G)**

8 Finally, with the knife angled horizontally, flush with the underside of the cake board, trim away any overhanging marzipan, moving the turntable around as you cut. **(H)**

9 Leave the cake to 'crust' for 8 hours or overnight before covering with sugarpaste.

covering a cake with modelling chocolate

When covering a cake with modelling chocolate, you can follow the same technique for covering a cake with marzipan, but modelling chocolate, especially dark modelling chocolate, can be quite firm to work with, particularly in colder weather. You can blitz it in the microwave on full power for intervals of ten seconds, checking whether it is soft enough to work with in between. If you over-zap it, simply pop it in the fridge to firm up again. If you don't have a microwave, you will have to cut it into small squares and, allowing the heat of your hands to warm it, knead it, piece by piece. Although this is time consuming, if your final design has a modelling chocolate finish (such as Midnight Lotus, see page 78) take comfort in the fact that you will only have to do this once, as modelling chocolate is stable enough not to require two layers. Use icing/confectioners' sugar for white chocolate and cocoa powder for dark chocolate when rolling out, to avoid streaking and stains. You can also, if you wish, cut the modelling chocolate 50/50 with sugar paste for a softer finish.

tip: to prevent sticking

You can avoid using too much icing/confectioners' sugar to prevent your chosen cake covering from sticking to the surface, by rolling it out on a large sheet of wax paper or baking parchment. You will still need a light dusting, but far less than if working directly onto the surface. Too much icing/confectioners' sugar can dry out sugar paste, making a smooth crack-free finish more difficult to achieve.

covering a cake with sugar paste

Sugar paste can be hard to work with if air bubbles get trapped inside. To avoid this, just keep folding the outside edges in and under when kneading, hiding all 'work' underneath.

1 Knead your sugar paste until it is soft and pliable and mould it into the correct shape for the cake you are covering – a ball for a round cake and a cube for a square cake. Working quickly, brush your cake with jam, alcohol or cooled boiled water before you start rolling, so your sugar paste isn't left to get dry. **(A)**

2 On a surface lightly dusted with icing/confectioners' sugar, roll out the sugar paste evenly to around 5 mm/¼ inch thick. Ensure that the sheet is large enough and that you have a good few inches of excess at the edges so you can avoid any folds or pleats. Rub a cake paddle over the surface to smooth it over, before picking it up with the rolling pin and carefully unfurling over the cake. **(B)**

3 Smooth the flat of your hand over the top of the cake to ensure the sugar paste has firmly adhered. Working on small sections at a time, smooth the sugar paste onto the sides of the cake, working downwards. If you find you have created a fold or a pleat, gently but quickly, lift that section of sugar paste and re-drape it, cupping as you do to prevent any trapped bubbles of air **(C)** then smooth the paddles over the cake to ensure a neat finish. **(D)**

4 Trim off most of the excess **(E)**, then lift the cake onto a turntable. Glide the cake paddles around the sides of the cake once more to ensure straight edges, but be careful not to drag the icing downwards as you will cause the sugar paste to crack and tear. **(F)**

5 Use a very sharp, small knife to trim off any extra icing that has been drawn lower than the cake board edge, keeping the knife flush with the board. This will ensure that your icing doesn't billow out towards the bottom of each tier. Once you have tidied the bottom edge, run the cake paddles around one final time. **(G)** Leave the cake to 'crust' for 8 hours or overnight before decorating.

If you are covering a square cake **(H)**, refer to the tip box on page 29 for advice on shaping the corners.

filling and covering small cakes

The method for covering small cakes with sugar paste is similar to that for larger cakes, except you do not need to cover them in marzipan first, although, of course, you can if you wish.

1 Using the relevant sized cutter, cut out rounds of sponge from your cake. **(A)** You will need 2 rounds per small cake for the Film Noir design (see page 75) and 3 rounds per cake for Something Borrowed... (see page 91).

2 Attach the first disc of cake to a cake board the same size as the disc with a little buttercream **(B)**, and use a small palette knife to smooth a generous layer of filling over the disc. **(C)** Place a second disc of cake on top and add another layer of buttercream. If you are making the Film Noir cakes, this will be your top layer; if you are making the miniatures for Something Borrowed..., add a third cake disc and smooth more buttercream over the top.

3 Smooth more buttercream over the sides and top of the cake, using a palette knife to really get the edges smooth **(D)**, then pop the cakes in the fridge to firm up for about 15 minutes.

4 Check to see whether the buttercream is still sticky enough for the icing to stick. If it's not, quickly brush over the top and sides with an appropriate flavoured alcohol or cooled boiled water (or, if, as in the photo, you are using pistachio and orange blossom cake, you can use orange blossom water).

5 Roll out the sugar paste until it is large enough to cover the cake, then rub a cake paddle over the top to smooth it out. Gently lift it onto your rolling pin and carefully unfurl it onto your cake. **(E)**

6 Quickly pat the sugar paste down and use your hands to cup the cake to ensure the sugar paste has adhered, then use your cake paddles to smooth the top and sides of the cake. **(F)** Lift the cake onto a small upturned glass or eggcup and trim off most of the excess with a small, sharp knife. **(G)**

7 Use the paddles again to make sure the sides are nice and straight **(H)** before trimming off the excess sugar paste, ensuring you keep the knife flush with the cake board. Leave the sugar paste to 'crust' for 8 hours or overnight before decorating.

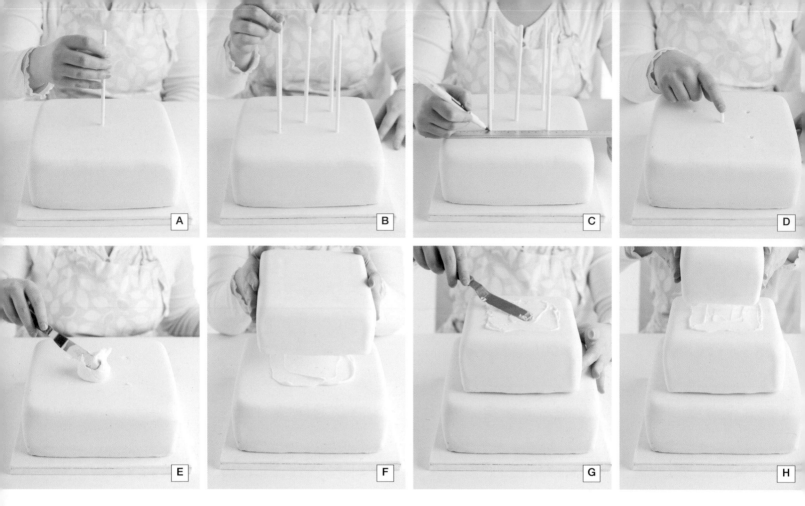

rodding and stacking a cake

Multi-tiered cakes need internal support to hold the weight of the cakes placed above them, and so the base two tiers will need to be rodded. This is not a corner that can be cut, as, without rodding, the top tiers will cave into the bottom tiers and the whole wedding cake could collapse. All established wedding venues and caterers know to expect rods inside multi-tiered cakes, which need to be removed before cutting. If a friend or family member, who has no prior experience of what to expect, has the task of cutting up and serving your wedding cake, make sure they are told beforehand that they will need to remove the rods before portioning it up.

YOU WILL NEED:

½ quantity Royal Icing (see page 20)

an iced cake drum and the 3 iced tiers of your cake

10 plastic dowelling rods (or more, if your cake is has more than 3 tiers)

a clean ruler

an edible ink pen

a hacksaw

sandpaper

1 Smooth a generous blob of royal icing over the centre of the iced cake drum. Place the base tier of your cake in the centre and use a cake paddle to gently push the cake down to help it stick and to close any gap between the cake and the board.

2 Push a dowelling rod into the centre of the base tier. **(A)** Insert a further 4 rods in a square around your central rod, making sure they are close enough to support and be hidden by the cake above. **(B)**

3 Line up the rods with a ruler and use the edible ink pen to mark on the rods where they meet the sugar paste/modelling chocolate. **(C)** Remove the rods and cut them down with a hacksaw (you can rub their tips with sandpaper if you need to smooth their tops). Wash and dry the rods before re-inserting them. **(D)**

4 Smooth a generous blob of icing over the centre of the cake **(E)** and place the next tier on top. **(F)** Use a cake paddle to gently press the middle tier down to close any gap between the cakes.

5 Repeat the rodding process with the middle tier **(G)**, before placing on the top tier. **(H)** Leave the cakes to set for a few minutes before moving them.

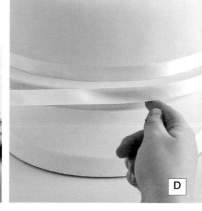

attaching a ribbon

Wrapping ribbons around the base of each tier and the cake drum ensures a smart, clean finish. By following my instructions for covering your cakes carefully with icing, you shouldn't have experienced any problems, but if you did run into difficulties, don't panic. Ribbon is an amateur wedding cake baker's best friend, covering, as it can, a multitude of sins. If you haven't quite managed to create the flawless finish you'd hoped for, you can always use a wider ribbon than those displayed in any of my designs if you need to. The decorations can hide the rest!

1 Place your iced, rodded and stacked cake on a turntable before you begin. Wrap your chosen ribbon around each tier, one at a time, to measure how long each length will need to be, leaving a little overlap. Cut the ribbon to length with fabric scissors.

2 Choose the least attractive view of your cake (if there is one!) as the back and attach one end of the ribbon with a small blob of royal icing. **(A)** Wrap the ribbon, quite tautly, around the cake and secure it in place with another small blob of royal icing. **(B)** Repeat with the remaining tiers, making sure all the ribbon joins are at the back.

3 For the cake drum, scrape a non-toxic glue stick around the edge (it's easier if the glue stick remains stationary while you turn the turntable). **(C)** Stick the ribbon around it **(D)** and your cake is ready to decorate.

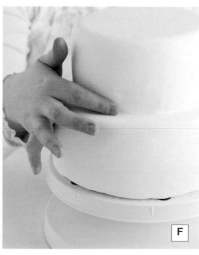

tip: an alternative to ribbon

If you don't like the look of ribbons around the base of your cakes and don't like the fuss of intricate piping borders, there is another way. You can create a clean line at the base of each tier by quickly piping a ring of royal icing into the tiny gap that is invariably present at the joining point of each tier. **(E)** Once you have piped the ring, use your index finger to smooth over the royal icing to flatten it, creating a seamless finish. **(F)**

A

B

C

D

making paper piping bags

You can buy ready-made silicone paper piping bags, but they're expensive, especially considering how easy they are to make. I have personally always preferred to use disposable plastic piping bags, as I find them more comfortable to hold and I also find the icing stays fresher for longer. Although, admittedly, they are a less environmentally friendly option, an added bonus is that when using very dark coloured royal icing, a plastic piping bag provides extra protection against your hands getting dyed. Which type of piping bag you use is personal choice, but do try piping with these first, as they are a far more economical and ecological choice. I would not recommend that you buy re-usable fabric piping bags, as they tend to get permanently dyed and are far less hygienic than disposable ones.

1 Take a large square sheet of baking parchment and cut it in half to make 2 equilateral triangles. **(A)**

2 Take one triangle and place it in front of you with the longest edge facing towards you. Pick up the bottom righthand corner edge of the triangle and turn it inwards to meet the centre point of the triangle. **(B)**

3 Bring the lefthand corner over the front of the bag all the way round to the back of the piping bag to meet the 2 central points, so they all line up and make a cone. **(C)**

4 Make sure the bag is taut and all the points line up **(D)**, then press the triangle flat and fold the protruding edge of the piping bag over on itself to keep the bag together. **(E)**

5 Cut the tip off the piping bag **(F)** and drop an icing nozzle/tip into the bag.

6 Holding the bag like a cone, spoon in royal icing until it reaches halfway up – no more, or it will squeeze out of the top of the bag while you're piping.

7 Fold and roll the top of the bag down until it is secure and your bag is ready to be used for piping.

E

F

piping techniques

Good piping starts with holding the piping bag correctly. Never overfill your piping bag as it will be much more likely to split, and never squeeze it in the middle or you'll get more icing on your arm than on your cake. Hold the piping bag in whichever hand feels most natural (usually the hand you write with) and use your thumb to apply downward pressure at the rolled up end of the bag. It will be this thumb that dictates the pressure of the icing flow. **(A)**

Use your index finger to help guide you and use your middle finger to support the bag from underneath – a bit like holding a syringe. Your other hand won't be left to sit idle though; it needs to act as a support platform for your piping hand. Without this support platform, the accuracy and fluidity of your piping will suffer. Your other hand needs to support your piping hand at the base, or, if you can rest your piping hand elsewhere, it can support and help guide your nozzle – this is particularly useful when piping on the top tier of a high cake, to prevent you leaning heavily on your cake and damaging it.

Piping is all about pressure and contact. You need to think about when to apply pressure and how much, as well as when to release it, while simultaneously concentrating on which areas to make contact with the cake and whether you need to maintain that contact or lift your nozzle/tip. The other crucial thing to remember is to keep your nozzle/tip clean. I always keep a slightly damp cloth and a few pieces of dry kitchen paper nearby, so that I have what I need at hand and can keep wiping my nozzle/tip to prevent it getting crusty.

The simplest technique to master is piping dots or pearls. **(B)** (See Grace Kelly on page 45 for full instructions.) This can be achieved with any sized nozzle/tip to create different sized pearls, but the more pressure you apply the bigger they will be. The same technique can be applied with a star nozzle/tip to create cute little royal icing stars. Once you gain confidence you can move on to piping swags **(C)** (see Versailles on page 54), and vertical lines **(D)** (see Brighton Rock on page 107).

Once you have mastered these basic techniques, you can move on to pressure piping. This is where the design is applied with the nozzle/tip in near constant contact with the cake surface **(E)** (see Art Nouveau on page 84), rather than by making initial contact before lifting your nozzle/tip and reattaching it at a different point (when the icing line falls into place on its own). Pressure piping is a more advanced skill, so if you are inexperienced, a few practice sessions will certainly help. Although trickier to perfect, don't be frightened to have a go. You may find that you take to it like a duck to water.

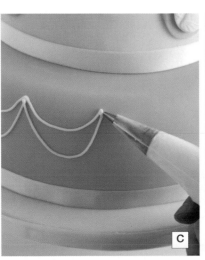

classic elegance

Inspired by style icons of the past, soft lace and feminine grace,
the wedding cakes in this chapter are refined, timeless creations,
perfect for couples seeking traditional style with a clean,
contemporary feel. With a focus on romance and
understatement, I have used soft, muted colours and simple lines.
Subtlety leads the way, with beautifully polished and tasteful
finesse: tradition without a hint of fustiness.

Broadway Melody

75 g/½ cup currants

100 g/⅔ cup sultanas/
golden raisins

150 g/1 cup seedless raisins

25 g/2½ tablespoons dried
sour cherries or dried
cranberries

75 g/2½ oz. pitted Medjool
dates, snipped into 3 with
kitchen scissors

50 g/⅓ cup natural glacé/
candied cherries, drained
and chopped in half

3 balls of Chinese stem
ginger, finely chopped

75 ml/5 tablespoons
brandy or dark rum, plus
1 tablespoon for steeping
(and more if maturing,
see step 12)

1 tablespoon espresso

1 teaspoon vanilla extract

grated zest and freshly
squeezed juice of 1 large
orange

75 g/5 tablespoons unsalted
butter, softened

50 g/¼ cup packed
molasses sugar

1 large egg, separated

125 g/1 cup plain/
all-purpose flour, sifted

1 teaspoon ground
cinnamon

1 teaspoon ground ginger

2 teaspoons mixed/apple-
pie spice

½ teaspoon freshly grated
nutmeg

50 g/½ cup ground almonds

a pinch of salt

a pinch of bicarbonate
of soda/baking soda

1 teaspoon water

100 g/⅓ cup apricot jam

*a 13-cm/5-inch deep square
cake pan*

*brown parcel paper and
kitchen string*

*a thin square cake board the
same size as the cake*

Exuding 1930s Hollywood glamour, this cake brings to mind images of Fred Astaire and Ginger Rogers, spinning across the dance floor in an elegantly choreographed routine. This refined and simple design will perfectly suit a sophisticated wedding with a touch of vintage charm. I have paired Broadway Melody with a classic Victorian fruitcake, full of plump, boozy fruit and warming spice. Deliciously moist and decadent, my fruitcake adds the perfect touch of tradition to any wedding, either as a single flavour option or as a top tier to save. This recipe is also the perfect choice for a Christmas or Christening cake.

TO MAKE THE VICTORIAN FRUITCAKE

Following the method below, prepare all 3 tiers of your cake, following the chart on page 141 to determine quantities, pan sizes and cooking times.

1 Grease, then double-line your cake pan with baking parchment and wrap brown paper around the outside of the pan, securing with string (this will help prevent the sides overcooking).

2 Pick off any unwanted stalks from the dried fruit. This is a laborious task, but it's well worth the effort to ensure your cake won't have a gritty texture.

3 Put the currants, sultanas/golden raisins, seedless raisins, sour cherries, dates, glacé/candied cherries and stem ginger in a saucepan with the brandy or rum and espresso. Place a sheet of baking parchment over the top of the saucepan before popping the lid on. Set the pan over a gentle heat and leave to simmer for 10–15 minutes, slowly bringing to the boil.

4 Remove the lid and baking parchment and quickly add the vanilla extract and the orange zest and juice. Stir the mixture over the heat until the liquid has mostly absorbed, then remove from the heat and leave to cool.

5 Preheat the oven to 160°C (145°C fan)/325°F (300°F fan)/Gas 3.

6 In a large mixing bowl and using an electric whisk, cream together the butter and sugar until pale and fluffy. Whisk in the egg yolk before folding in the flour, spices, ground almonds and salt. Tip in your cooled fruit mixture, along with any remaining liquid, and mix thoroughly.

7 In a separate, spotlessly clean bowl, whisk the egg white until it forms soft peaks. Dissolve the bicarbonate of soda/baking soda in the water, then whisk into your egg white.

8 Fold the egg white into the cake batter with a large metal spoon, being careful not to beat the air out of the mixture.

9 Spoon the batter into your prepared cake pan and gently smooth the top with a palette knife. Trickle a little water over the surface of the cake and pat it evenly over the top of the mixture with

your fingers. (This helps prevent the top browning too quickly.) Pop the cake in the preheated oven and bake for 1 hour, then cover the top of the cake with baking parchment or foil, turn the oven temperature down to 150°C (135°C fan)/300°F (275°F fan)/ Gas 2, and leave to bake for a further 75 minutes. (If following this method for larger cakes, refer to the chart on page 141 for specific cooking times.)

10 To check the cake is fully baked, insert a skewer into the middle of the cake and leave it there for 30 seconds before removing. If the skewer comes out clean, the cake is baked. If the skewer has any remaining sticky residue, return to the oven and check again after 10 minutes.

11 Once baked, place the warm cake, still in its pan, on a wire rack and stab it all over with a skewer. Pour the brandy or rum reserved for steeping over

the top of the cake, then leave it to cool completely in its pan before turning out.

12 The cake will be delicious if covered and eaten immediately, or you can let it mature for 6–8 weeks. To mature, wrap your cold cake in a layer of baking parchment and then a layer of foil before transferring to an airtight container. Once a week for 6–8 weeks, unwrap your cake and pour over a little more brandy or rum (see page 141 for quantities based on your cake size). After steeping, carefully rewrap the cake and place back in the airtight container.

13 When you are ready to decorate the cake, boil then sieve/strain the apricot jam, following the instructions on page 27. Brush it over the cake board and place the cake onto it, then brush the rest of the cake with the jam and proceed directly to the decorating instructions below.

---

tip: the ribbon and bow

The total weight of sugar paste mixed half-and-half with floristry paste that you will need to make the edible ribbon and bow will depend on the size of your cake tiers. As a helpful guide, I have broken down the quantities you will need for the various cake sizes individually, so that you can simply add up the quantities for the tier sizes you have chosen. First of all, you will need approximately 250 g/9 oz. for the bow (that's 125 g/4½ oz. of sugar paste and 125 g/4½ oz. of floristry paste, kneaded together), and this will be the same for whichever size tiers you have. For the ribbons, you will need 250 g/9 oz. to go around a square 13-cm/5-inch cake, 350 g/ 12 oz. for an 18-cm/7-inch, 400 g/14 oz. for a 20-cm/8-inch, 450 g/1 lb. for a 23-cm/9-inch and 550 g/1¼ lbs. for a 28-cm/11-inch cake.

FOR THE DECORATION

marzipan (see page 157 for quantities)

ivory sugar paste (see page 157 for quantities)

a cake drum 8 cm/3 inches larger than the base tier

1.5-cm/¾-inch wide white satin ribbon

pearl edible lustre spray

white sugar paste and floristry paste (see tip box)

icing/confectioners' sugar, for dusting

clear alcohol (such as vodka)

1 quantity Royal Icing (see page 20)

snowflake and antique gold edible lustre dusts

rejuvenator fluid

a ruler or tape measure

a wheel tool

a small paintbrush

4-cm/1½-inch, 3-cm/ 1¼-inch and 2-cm/¾-inch round cutters

a piping bag fitted with a fine round nozzle/tip

TO DECORATE THE CAKE

1 Cover your 3 cake tiers with marzipan followed by sugarpaste, then cover your cake drum in the same ivory sugar paste (refer to pages 26 and 28–30 for full instructions). Rod and stack the cake (following the instructions on page 32).

2 Spray the satin ribbon with pearl lustre and leave to dry, then attach it to the edge of the cake drum (see page 33).

3 Measure the circumference of each tier and jot down – these will be the lengths you'll need to cut the sugar-paste ribbon to.

4 Combine the sugar and floristry pastes and knead together into a ball. On a surface dusted with icing/ confectioners' sugar, roll out a large piece of the paste to a strip long enough to wrap around the top tier. (Store any that you aren't using in a plastic bag so it doesn't dry out.) Using a wheel tool and ruler, neatly trim the strip to 2.5 cm/1 inch wide. **(A)**

5 Place the strip on a piece of baking parchment and spray it generously with pearl lustre. **(B)**

6 Paint the base of the top tier with a little alcohol **(C)** and attach the sugar-paste ribbon to the cake. **(D)**

7 Repeat steps 4–6 to ribbon the middle and base tiers.

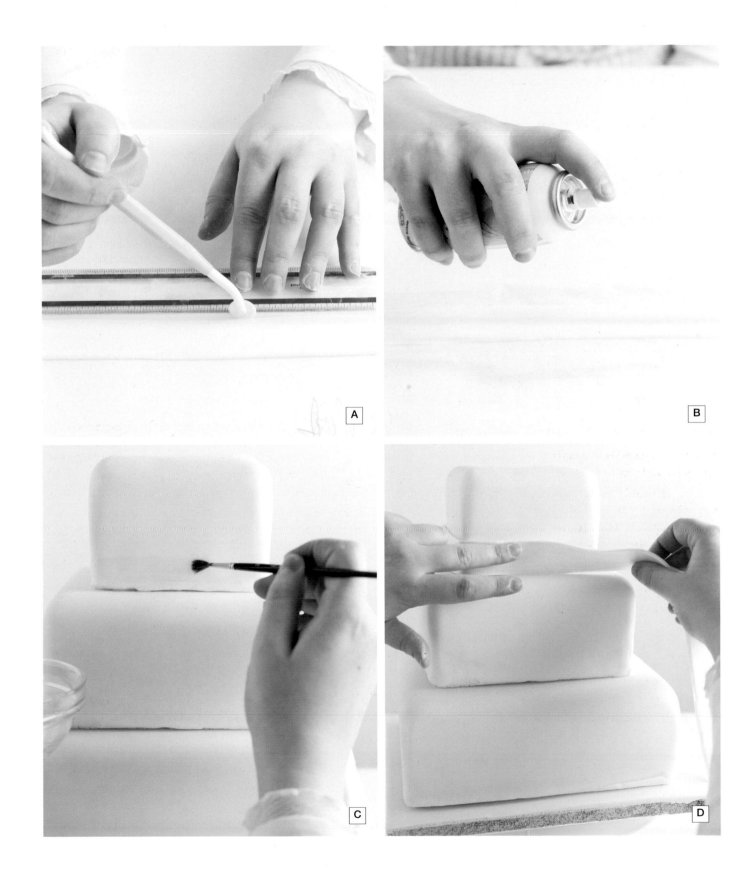

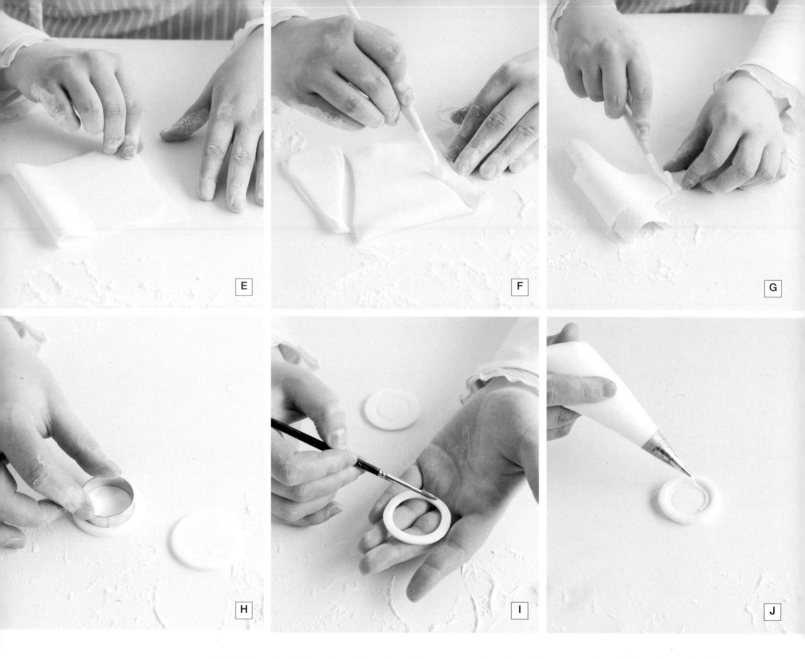

E

F

G

H

I

J

8 Next, knead and roll out another piece of sugar and floristry paste to a rectangle about 20 cm/8 inches long and 10 cm/4 inches wide. Liberally dust the top of the rectangle with icing/confectioners' sugar and gently fold in half to make a square, but do not press down on the fold. **(E)**

9 Use the wheel tool to cut a curve into each side of the square. **(F)** Open it out again and you should be left with an eye-shaped piece of icing. Tidy any uneven edges with the wheel tool.

10 Roll a piece of kitchen paper towel into a sausage shape and position it in the centre of the eye before folding one narrow end over to meet

the other. The paper will enable the bow to hold its shape while it sets. If the loop of the bow seems a little too long, trim the end with a wheel tool. **(G)** Repeat to create the other side of the bow. Place the bow pieces on a piece of baking parchment and spray generously with pearl lustre.

11 Knead and roll out another piece of paste, and stamp out two 4-cm/1½-inch circles with the cutter, then use the 3-cm/1¼-inch cutter to stamp a smaller circle out of the centre of one of those. **(H)**

12 Use the 2-cm/¾-inch cutter and press gently into the centre of the other 4-cm/1½-inch circle to make an impression.

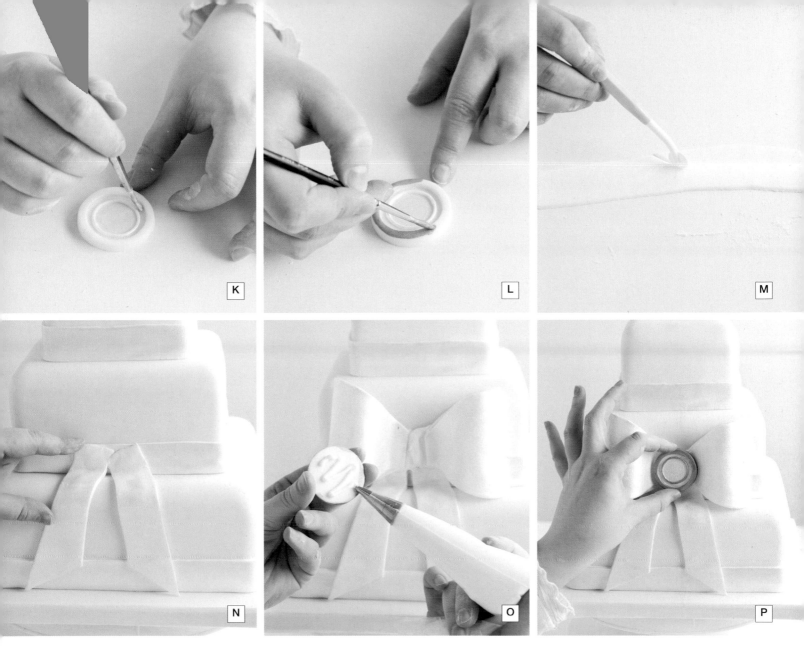

13 Paint alcohol around the edge of the 4-cm/1-inch ring **(I)** and place it on top of the other 4-cm/1-inch circle to give the brooch a raised rim.

14 Fill the piping bag with royal icing and pipe around the circle impression in the centre of the brooch **(J)**, then leave the pieces to dry overnight.

15 When the brooch is dry, mix snowflake lustre dust with a little rejuvenator fluid in a small bowl and use it to paint the inside of the brooch. **(K)**

16 Once dry, gild the piped ring and rim of the brooch with a little antique gold lustre dust mixed with rejuvenator fluid. **(L)**

17 Create the ribbon ends for the bow in the same way that you created the ribbons, rolling 2.5-cm/ 1-inch wide strips, then cutting the ends diagonally for a pretty finish. **(M)** Spray with pearl lustre.

18 Attach the ribbon ends to the ribbon of the middle tier, using royal icing. **(N)**

19 Once all the components of the bow have dried, position each side of the bow loop on top of the ribbon ends, affixing with royal icing.

20 To finish, pipe a little royal icing onto the back of the brooch **(O)** and secure it in the centre of the bow with a flourish! **(P)**

Grace Kelly

No one has epitomized style and glamour more effortlessly than Grace Kelly. This stunning cake follows her lead with understated elegance and feminine beauty; the delicate pearls shimmer with iridescent lustre and catch the light, adding to the mood of romance. I have paired this design with a moist chocolate fudge cake filled with a rich chocolate buttercream.

TO MAKE THE CHOCOLATE FUDGE CAKE

Following the method below, prepare all 3 tiers of your cake, following the chart on page 142 to determine quantities, pan sizes and cooking times.

1 Preheat the oven to 180°C (160°C fan)/350°F (325°F fan)/Gas 4.

2 Put the chocolate, milk and a third of the sugar in a saucepan set over a gentle heat. Stir until the chocolate and sugar have melted, then remove from the heat and leave to cool slightly.

3 In a large mixing bowl, cream together the butter and the remaining sugar until pale and fluffy. Gradually beat in the eggs, followed by the vanilla and salt, then whisk in the chocolate milk. Sift the dry ingredients over the batter and fold in gently.

4 Divide the batter between your cake pans and bake in the preheated oven for about 25 minutes, or until an inserted skewer comes out clean.

5 Leave the cakes to cool in their pans, set on a wire rack, for 10 minutes before turning out onto the rack to cool completely.

6 To make the buttercream, whisk the butter for a few seconds until pale and creamy, then sift over half of the icing/confectioners' sugar and whisk again until all combined. Add the melted and cooled chocolate and whisk through before sifting over the remaining icing/confectioners' sugar. Whisk for a few minutes, adding a splash of milk to slightly slacken the buttercream, if you need to.

7 Level the cakes, if necessary (see page 25), then attach one of the cakes to the cake board with a small blob of buttercream. Sandwich the cakes together with half of the buttercream, then spread the remaining buttercream over the top and sides of the cake with a palette knife (see page 27) and leave to set.

FOR A 20-CM/8-INCH CAKE

100 g/3½ oz. good quality (70% cocoa solids) dark chocolate, broken into pieces

200 ml/¾ cup whole milk

225 g/1 cup packed plus 2 tablespoons light muscovado sugar

75 g/5 tablespoons unsalted butter, softened

2 large eggs, beaten

2 teaspoons vanilla extract, or to taste

a pinch of salt

125 g/1 cup plain/all-purpose flour

25 g/3 tablespoons unsweetened cocoa powder

1 teaspoon bicarbonate of soda/baking soda

FOR THE RICH CHOCOLATE BUTTERCREAM

100 g/6½ tablespoons unsalted butter, softened

175 g/1¼ cups icing/confectioners' sugar

100 g/3½ oz. good quality (70% cocoa solids) dark chocolate, melted and cooled

a splash of milk (optional)

2 x 20-cm/8-inch shallow round cake pans, greased and lined

a thin round cake board the same size as the cake

FOR THE DECORATION

marzipan (see page 157 for quantities)

white sugar paste (see page 157 for quantities)

a cake drum 8 cm/3 inches larger than the base tier

1.5-cm/¾-inch wide white satin ribbon

1 quantity Royal Icing (see page 20)

snowflake and champagne edible lustre dusts

rejuvenator fluid

a piping bag fitted with a medium–fine nozzle/tip

a cake turntable

a small paintbrush

TO DECORATE THE CAKE

1 Cover your 3 cake tiers with marzipan followed by sugarpaste, then cover your cake drum in the same white sugar paste (refer to pages 26 and 28–30 for full instructions).

2 Rod and stack the cake (following the instructions on page 32), then ribbon the cake and the cake drum (see page 33).

3 Fill the piping bag with the royal icing and place your prepared cake on a turntable. Starting with the top tier, just above the ribbon, pipe even sized pearls in rows of between 1 and 5, all the way around the cake. **(A)** To create a pearl, hold your bag so that the nozzle/tip is facing, head-on, the point on the cake that you want to ice, without actually touching it. Gently apply a little pressure with your thumb at a steady rate. Once you have created a pearl of the desired size, release the pressure and remove the nozzle quickly. If you have unwanted high peaks on your pearls, you can use a paintbrush dampened with water to smooth them out.

4 Once you have created an initial line of pearls, continue to pipe more randomly. Think of falling raindrops, or the game Tetris. There should be more pearls gathered at the bottom of the tier, so the top of each cake will be less crowded with pearls. **(B)**

5 Continue piping randomly with single and joined groups of pearls over the top of the cake.

6 Repeat the process all around the sides of the middle and base tiers, then pipe a few pearls on the iced cake drum for design unity. By the time you have finished piping the cake drum, the top tier will have set and be ready to be hand painted.

7 In a small bowl, mix half and half of snowflake and champagne lustre dusts. Add enough rejuvenator fluid to the lustre powder to create a paint, then mix together with the paintbrush. **(C)**

8 Carefully dab each piped pearl with the lustre. **(D)** You really don't need very much so don't overload your paintbrush or you may risk it dripping onto the white icing. As you work, the alcohol will evaporate from the lustre dust, so you will need to top it up every now and then with a little more rejuvenator fluid.

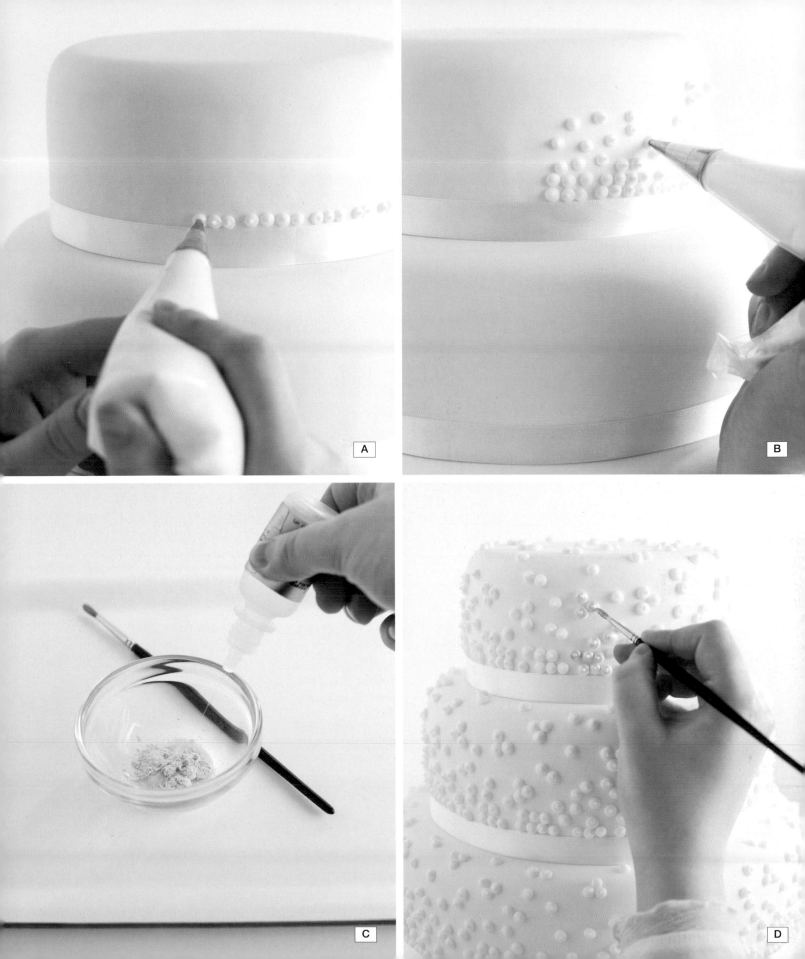

White on White

This pretty cake is a timeless classic. Pure white sugar paste decorated with delicate piping and adorned with dainty blossoms. Romantic and versatile, it is equally at home in a grand hotel as in a colourful, flower-filled garden. I have paired this design with red velvet cake, as I love the hidden drama of vibrant red beneath crisp white icing. Red velvet is a delightfully crumbly cake with a subtle hint of chocolate, generously filled with rich, vanilla cream cheese frosting.

TO MAKE THE RED VELVET CAKE

Following the method below, prepare all 3 tiers of your cake, following the chart on page 143 to determine quantities, pan sizes and cooking times.

1 Preheat the oven to 180°C (160°C fan)/350°F (325°F fan)/Gas 4.

2 In a large mixing bowl and using an electric whisk, cream together the butter and sugar until pale and fluffy. Add the egg yolks, one at a time, whisking between each addition, then whisk in the vanilla extract.

3 In a jug/pitcher, stir the red food colouring into the buttermilk. This will give you an indication of how red the cake will be, and it should be very red, so add more dye at this stage, if needed.

4 Combine the flour, cocoa and baking powder in a separate bowl. Sift a third of the flour mixture over the sugar, butter and eggs and whisk in, then pour in a third of the buttermilk and whisk again. Continue to add thirds of the dry and wet ingredients alternately, mixing well between each addition, until all the flour and buttermilk have been fully combined.

5 In a separate, spotlessly clean bowl and with clean beaters, whisk the egg whites with the salt until they form stiff peaks.

6 Vigorously beat 1 spoonful of the egg white into the cake batter to help slacken it, then gently fold in the remaining egg white with a metal spoon, being careful not to knock the air out of the mixture.

7 Mix the vinegar and bicarbonate of soda/baking soda together, then fold through the batter.

8 Divide the batter evenly between your prepared cake pans, level the surface with a palette knife and pop them in the preheated oven to bake for 25–30 minutes, or until an inserted skewer comes out clean.

9 Once baked, leave the cakes to cool in their pans, set on a wire rack, for 10 minutes before turning out onto the rack to cool completely.

10 To make the frosting, whisk together the butter and cream cheese until smooth and creamy. Sift over half the icing/confectioners' sugar and whisk to incorporate. Sift over the remaining icing/confectioners' sugar and whisk again until the mixture is creamy. This can take a couple of minutes, so be patient. Add the vanilla and whisk again. Taste for vanilla, whisking in more if needed.

11 Level the cakes, if necessary (see page 25), then attach one of the cakes to the cake board with a small blob of frosting. Sandwich the cakes together with half of the frosting, then spread the remaining frosting over the top and sides of the cake with a palette knife (see page 27) and leave to set.

FOR A 20-CM/8-INCH CAKE

200 g/1 stick plus 5 tablespoons unsalted butter, softened

200 g/1 cup (caster) sugar

2 large eggs, separated

1 tablespoon vanilla extract

2 teaspoons extra-red food colouring paste

250 ml/1 cup buttermilk

250 g/2 cups plain/all-purpose flour

20 g/2½ tablespoons unsweetened cocoa powder

1 teaspoon baking powder

¼ teaspoon salt

2 teaspoons white wine vinegar

1 teaspoon bicarbonate of soda/baking soda

FOR THE VANILLA CREAM CHEESE FROSTING

75 g/5 tablespoons unsalted butter, softened

75 g/5 tablespoons Philadelphia cream cheese (see page 4)

300 g/2 cups plus 2 tablespoons icing/confectioners' sugar

1½ tablespoons vanilla extract

2 x 20-cm/8-inch shallow round cake pans, greased and lined

a thin round cake board the same size as the cake

FOR THE DECORATION

marzipan (see page 157 for quantities)

white sugar paste (see page 157 for quantities)

a cake drum 8 cm/3 inches larger than the base tier

1.5-cm/¾-inch wide white satin ribbon

approx. 150 g/5½ oz. white floristry paste

cornflour/cornstarch, for dusting

1 quantity Royal Icing (see page 20)

13-mm/½-inch and 5-mm/¼-inch blossom plunge cutters

a ball tool

a moulded drying rack

a piping bag fitted with a very fine nozzle/tip

a piping bag fitted with a fine nozzle/tip

a soft brush

TO DECORATE THE CAKE

1 Cover your 3 cake tiers with marzipan followed by sugarpaste, then cover your cake drum in the same white sugar paste (refer to pages 26 and 28–30 for full instructions).

2 Rod and stack the cake (following the instructions on page 32), then ribbon the cake and the cake drum (see page 33).

3 Take a small piece of floristry paste and knead it until pliable. On a surface lightly dusted with cornflour/cornstarch, roll out the floristry paste very thinly.

4 Using the plunge cutters, punch out roughly 60 blossoms for a 15-cm/6-inch, 20-cm/8-inch, 25-cm/10-inch cake. **(A)** (You will need to adjust this number for a smaller or larger cake.) It's always useful to make more flowers than you need to include in your patch kit (see page 14), just in case any blossoms get chipped or fall off during delivery.

5 Using the fatter end of a ball tool, roll out each petal from the centre to create a more delicate finish. **(B)**

6 Place the blossoms on a moulded drying rack and impress the centre of each blossom with the thin end of the ball tool **(C)**, then leave to dry. (They begin to dry pretty quickly, so they don't need to be made too far ahead, but ideally leave them to air dry overnight.)

7 Spoon royal icing into the piping bag fitted with the very fine nozzle and draw wavering lines over the whole cake to create the stems for the blossoms to hang upon. **(D)**

tip: using floristry paste

Floristry paste is specially designed for modelling intricate decorations, such as flowers. It can be rolled extremely thinly, to create delicate and naturalistic results and sets like fine porcelain. It is a completely edible material, though the taste is a little less pleasant than sugar paste. Work with it in small amounts at a time – this stuff begins to dry out extremely quickly and, although you can use a cel flap (a special plastic sheet) to keep the paste moist for longer, I find working with it in small quantities gives more reliable results. Plus, it means one less piece of equipment you need to buy!

E

F

G

H

8 Affix the blossoms to the stems with a small blob of royal icing from the piping bag, dispersing them evenly over the cake. **(E)**

9 Fill the piping bag fitted with the fine nozzle/tip with royal icing and use it to pipe a single dot in the centre of each blossom. **(F)**

10 Continuing with the same piping bag, pipe leaves running down each stem. Pipe a single dot next to the stem, before releasing your thumb pressure and dragging the nozzle/tip away from the dot in the direction you want the leaf tip to be pointing. **(G)**

11 Return to the piping bag with the very fine nozzle/tip and finish the design by piping sets of 3 closely grouped dots around some of the blossoms. **(H)**

12 Finally, once the cake has completely set, dust it with a soft brush to remove any excess icing/confectioners' sugar or fibre flecks from the ribbons.

Versailles

This eye-catching, graceful cake is inspired by Marie-Antoinette at the Palace of Versailles. In pastel, macaron colours with intricately piped swags and bows and delicate cameos, this cake embodies feminine charm. Chic and original, Versailles is perfect for couples seeking classic elegance with a subtle splash of colour. I have paired this design with apple and Calvados cake with a toffee apple buttercream. Calvados is a decadently delicious French apple brandy that elevates this cake from comforting farmhouse sponge to an indulgent treat fit for this most special of celebrations.

FOR A 15-CM/6-INCH CAKE

50 g/⅓ cup sultanas/golden raisins

90 ml/6 tablespoons Calvados

2 sharp, sweet eating apples (Pink Lady, Jazz and Braeburn are all excellent)

150 g/¾ cup packed light muscovado sugar

100 g/¾ cup self-raising flour

1 teaspoon baking powder

50 g/½ cup ground almonds

150 g/1 stick plus 2 tablespoons unsalted butter, softened

3 large eggs

½ teaspoon freshly grated nutmeg

a pinch of salt

a splash of milk (optional)

FOR THE BUTTERSCOTCH

25 g/2 tablespoons light muscovado sugar

1 tablespoon salted butter

FOR THE TOFFEE BUTTERCREAM

25 g/1½ tablespoons salted butter, softened

25 g/2 tablespoons light muscovado sugar

2 tablespoons Calvados

75 g/5 tablespoons unsalted butter, softened

150 g/1 cup icing/confectioners' sugar

2 x 15-cm/6-inch shallow round cake pans, greased and lined

a thin round cake board the same size as the cake

TO MAKE THE APPLE AND CALVADOS CAKE

Following the method below, prepare all 3 tiers of your cake, following the chart on page 144 to determine quantities, pan sizes and cooking times.

1 Put the sultanas/golden raisins in a shallow bowl and pour over the Calvados. Cover the bowl in cling film/plastic wrap and leave them to plump up for about half an hour, then drain and set aside, reserving the soaking Calvados for the butterscotch.

2 Wash, halve and core the apples, then slice each half into 4.

3 To make the butterscotch, put the sugar and reserved soaking Calvados in a deep frying pan. Stir over a gentle heat until the sugar dissolves, then turn up the heat slightly and continue to heat until the syrup turns to a soft caramel. Add the salted butter and stir until melted.

4 Place the apples in the butterscotch pan, flesh-side down. Turn the heat down and leave them to simmer for about 10 minutes, until the apples soften, turning them over occasionally so they are fully coated in the butterscotch. Using a slotted spoon, remove the apples from the butterscotch and place them on a cold dish to cool, reserving the butterscotch for later. Once cooled, chop the apples into chunky pieces.

5 Preheat the oven to 170°C (150°C fan)/325°F (300°F fan)/Gas 3.

6 In a large mixing bowl and using an electric whisk, cream together the sugar, flour, baking powder, almonds, butter, eggs, nutmeg and salt, until you have a light, fluffy batter. You can add a splash of milk if the consistency is a bit too stiff, but you don't want it to be too loose or all your apple pieces will sink to the bottom of the cake.

7 Once the batter is thoroughly mixed, add the chopped apples and drained sultanas and fold them in with a metal spoon.

8 Pour the batter into your prepared cake pans and bake on the middle shelf of the preheated oven for about 40–45 minutes, or until an inserted

skewer comes out clean. If the tops of the cakes are starting to brown too quickly, lay a sheet of foil over the top of each cake for the second half of the cooking time.

9 Once baked, place the warm cakes, still in their pans, on a wire rack and stab them all over with a skewer. Pour the reserved butterscotch over the cakes, then leave them to cool completely in their pans before turning out. (If the butterscotch has started to solidify, you can warm it over a gentle heat to loosen it up.)

10 To make the flavouring for the buttercream, put the salted butter, sugar and Calvados in a small saucepan set over a gentle heat and stir until everything has melted. Increase the heat and boil for a few minutes until the liquid thickens to a smooth toffee sauce, then remove from the heat and leave to cool completely.

11 Whisk the unsalted butter until soft. Sift over half the icing/confectioners' sugar and whisk again until thoroughly combined.

12 Add the cooled toffee sauce to the buttercream and whisk in, then sift over the remaining icing/confectioners' sugar and continue to whisk until soft and creamy.

13 Level the cakes, if necessary (see page 25), then attach one of the cakes to the cake board with a small blob of buttercream. Sandwich the cakes together with half of the buttercream, then spread the remaining buttercream over the top and sides of the cake with a palette knife (see page 27) and leave to set.

TO DECORATE THE CAKE

FOR THE DECORATION

marzipan (see page 157 for quantities)

powder pink sugar paste (see page 157 for quantities), plus a little extra for the cameos

ivory sugar paste (see page 157 for quantities)

a cake drum 8 cm/3 inches larger than the base tier

1.5-cm/¾-inch wide white satin ribbon

approx. 100 g/3½ oz. white floristry paste

cornflour/cornstarch, for dusting

clear alcohol (such as vodka)

1 quantity Royal Icing (see page 20)

a silicone cameo mould

a round cutter slightly larger than the cameo mould

a small paintbrush

a piping bag fitted with a fine round nozzle/tip

a piping bag fitted with a medium–fine nozzle/tip

1 Cover your 3 cake tiers with marzipan (you can brush the cake with more Calvados to stick on the marzipan if the buttercream is too set), then cover the top and base tiers in pink sugar paste and the middle tier and cake drum in ivory sugar paste (refer to pages 26 and 28–30 for full instructions).

2 Rod and stack the cake (following the instructions on page 32), then ribbon the cake and the cake drum (see page 33).

3 To make the cameos, knead a small piece of the floristry paste until pliable, then roll it into a ball and dust it with cornflour/cornstarch, before firmly pushing it into the cameo mould. Pass a rolling pin over the top of the mould to flatten the back of the cameo and ensure it is an even depth **(A)**, then carefully turn the cameo out of the mould. **(B)**

4 Roll out a small ball of pink sugar paste and use the round cutter to cut out a disc. **(C)** Roll over the disc with a rolling pin, in one direction only, to create an oval shape.

5 Paint a little alcohol on the back of the cameo **(D)** and affix to the pink oval. **(E)** Repeat to make at least 7 cameos in total (you will need more for a larger cake), then leave them to dry overnight.

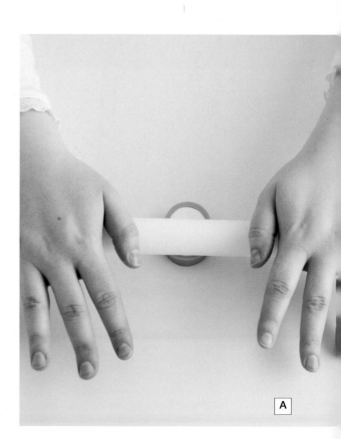

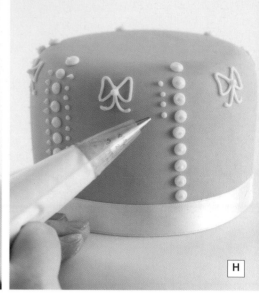

6 Fill the piping bag fitted with the fine nozzle/tip with royal icing and pipe 6 small bows around the top of the top tier cake, spacing them evenly. **(F)**

7 Fill the piping bag fitted with the medium–fine nozzle/tip with icing and pipe vertical lines of pearls between the bows. To create a pearl, hold your bag so that the nozzle/tip is facing, head-on, the point on the cake that you want to ice, without touching it and steadily apply pressure with your thumb. Once you have created a pearl of the desired size, release the pressure and remove the nozzle quickly. **(G)**

8 Using the piping bag fitted with the fine nozzle/tip, pipe a vertical row of small dots on either side of the line of large pearls. **(H)**

9 Pipe a line running from the side of one bow, over the top of the line of pearls, and back down until you reach the next bow edge. **(I)** Repeat this between the remaining bows.

10 Using a generous blob of royal icing on the back of each cameo, affix the cameos around the middle tier at regular intervals. **(J)**

11 Still using the fine nozzle/tip, pipe a double layer of swags around the base tier of the cake. To create a swag, you must first apply a little pressure to make contact with the cake surface and then, with continued even pressure, pull the icing in a string away from the cake before making contact again at the end. This will create a beautiful loop. **(K)**

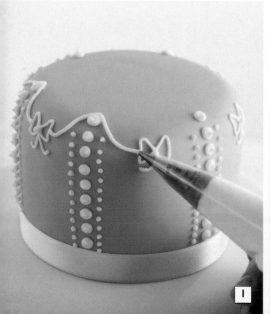

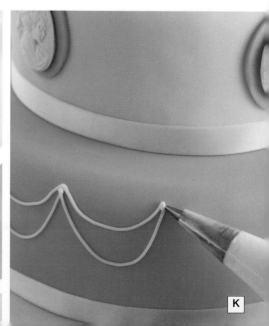

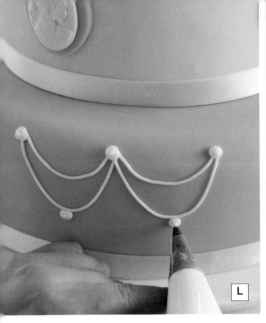

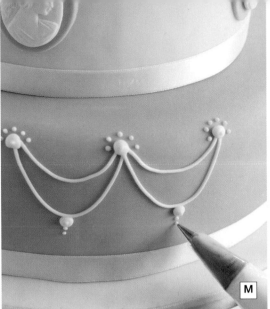

12 Using the piping bag with the medium–fine nozzle/tip, pipe a large pearl at the top of each swag, where they join, and another below the centre point of the lower swag. **(L)**

13 Return to the piping bag fitted with the fine nozzle/tip and pipe the finishing touches to the cake. Pipe an arch of 5 small dots around the large pearls at the tops of the swags, and 2 dots beneath the pearls at the base of the swags. **(M)**

14 Move up to the top of the cake and pipe a similar arch of 5 small dots around the top of each vertical line of pearls.

15 Finally, finish the cameos by piping an oval of small dots around each one. **(N)**

tip: piping guidance

If you struggle to pipe perfectly vertical lines and pearls, try creating a plumb line with a piece of kitchen string, to work as a guide. It can be kept in place on the top of the cake by weighting the end with a small cake drum.

Antique Lace

This stylish cake makes a beautiful centrepiece with its muted caramel icing and pearl-dusted lace appliqué. By recreating details from the bridal lace, this is the perfect cake with which to make a truly personal statement. You can buy ready-made lace moulds or you can create your own, simply and cheaply, using food-grade silicone for a tailor-made design. I have paired the Antique Lace design with a full-flavoured, moist and spicy ginger cake.

TO MAKE THE STICKY GINGER CAKE

Following the method below, prepare all 3 tiers of your cake, following the chart on page 145 to determine quantities, pan sizes and cooking times.

1 Preheat the oven to 160°C (145°C fan)/325°F (300°F fan)/Gas 3.

2 Melt the butter, molasses sugar and syrup in a large saucepan set over a gentle heat. Remove from

the heat and leave to cool for 5 minutes, then beat in the milk, egg and chopped ginger. Sift the flour, ground ginger and salt over the mixture and fold in until well combined.

3 Divide the batter evenly between the prepared cake pans and bake in the preheated oven for 30–35 minutes, or until an inserted skewer comes out clean.

4 Once baked, place the warm cakes, still in their pans, on a wire rack and stab them all over with a skewer. Spoon the ginger syrup over the cakes, then leave them to cool completely in their pans before turning out.

5 To make the buttercream, whisk the butter and ginger syrup together. Sift over half of the icing/confectioners' sugar and whisk until combined. Sift over the other half of the icing/confectioners' sugar and whisk again at a high speed until the buttercream is light and creamy (this can take a couple of minutes).

6 Level the cakes, if necessary (see page 25), then attach one of the cakes to the cake board with a small blob of buttercream. Sandwich the cakes together with half of the buttercream, then spread the remaining buttercream over the top and sides of the cake with a palette knife (see page 27) and leave to set.

FOR A 15-CM/6-INCH CAKE

100 g/6½ tablespoons unsalted butter, cubed

75 g/⅓ cup packed molasses sugar

3 tablespoons golden/light corn syrup

100 ml/⅓ cup whole milk

1 large egg, beaten

3 balls of Chinese stem ginger, finely chopped

125 g/1 cup self-raising flour

1 tablespoon ground ginger

¼ teaspoon salt

2 tablespoons ginger syrup*

FOR THE GINGER BUTTERCREAM

75 g/5 tablespoons unsalted butter, softened

3 tablespoons ginger syrup*

150 g/1 cup icing/confectioners' sugar

2 x 15-cm/6-inch shallow round cake pans, greased and lined

a thin round cake board the same size as the cake

* This can be drained from the stem ginger jar or you can make your own following the instructions on page 145.

FOR THE DECORATION

marzipan (see page 157 for quantities)

caramel-coloured sugar paste (see page 157 for quantities)

a cake drum 8 cm/3 inches larger than the base tier

1.5-cm/¾-inch wide white satin ribbon

2.5-cm/1-inch wide white lace ribbon

pearl edible lustre spray

1 quantity Royal Icing (see page 20)

approx 150 g/5½ oz. white sugarpaste

approx 150 g/5½ oz. white floristry paste

cornflour/cornstarch, for dusting

pearl edible lustre dust

rejuvenator fluid

a piping bag fitted with a small round nozzle/tip

a silicone lace mould

a wheel tool

a small paintbrush

TO DECORATE THE CAKE

1 Cover your 3 cake tiers with marzipan followed by sugarpaste, then cover your cake drum in the same caramel sugar paste (refer to pages 26 and 28–30 for full instructions).

2 Rod and stack the cake (following the instructions on page 32), then ribbon the cake drum with the white satin ribbon (see page 33).

3 Measure and cut a length of white lace ribbon to go around each cake tier and the cake drum. Spray each length with pearl lustre **(A)** and leave to dry.

4 Wrap lace ribbon around the cake drum (over the white satin ribbon), with the pearlized side out, and affix (see page 33).

5 Spoon the royal icing into the piping bag, then wrap each cake tier with the pearlized lace, securing each length with a blob of icing (see page 33).

6 Knead together half and half of white sugar paste and white floristry paste until pliable, then press the piece into your chosen silicone lace mould. **(B)**

7 Roll over the top of the mould with the rolling pin to ensure the lace is an even depth. **(C)**

8 Turn the lace out of the mould onto a surface lightly dusted with cornflour/cornstarch. **(D)**

9 Use a wheel tool to carefully cut around the edges of the lace, trimming off any excess icing. **(E)**

10 You can, if you wish, cut out individual details from each lace cast to make smaller pieces and give variation to your finished design. **(F)**

11 As you cut out the lace pieces, pipe royal icing onto the back of each **(G)** and attach them to the cake. **(H)** When the cake is covered in lace, leave it to set.

12 In a small bowl, mix pearl lustre dust with enough rejuvenator fluid to create a paint. Carefully paint the lace pieces with the solution and leave to dry. **(I)**

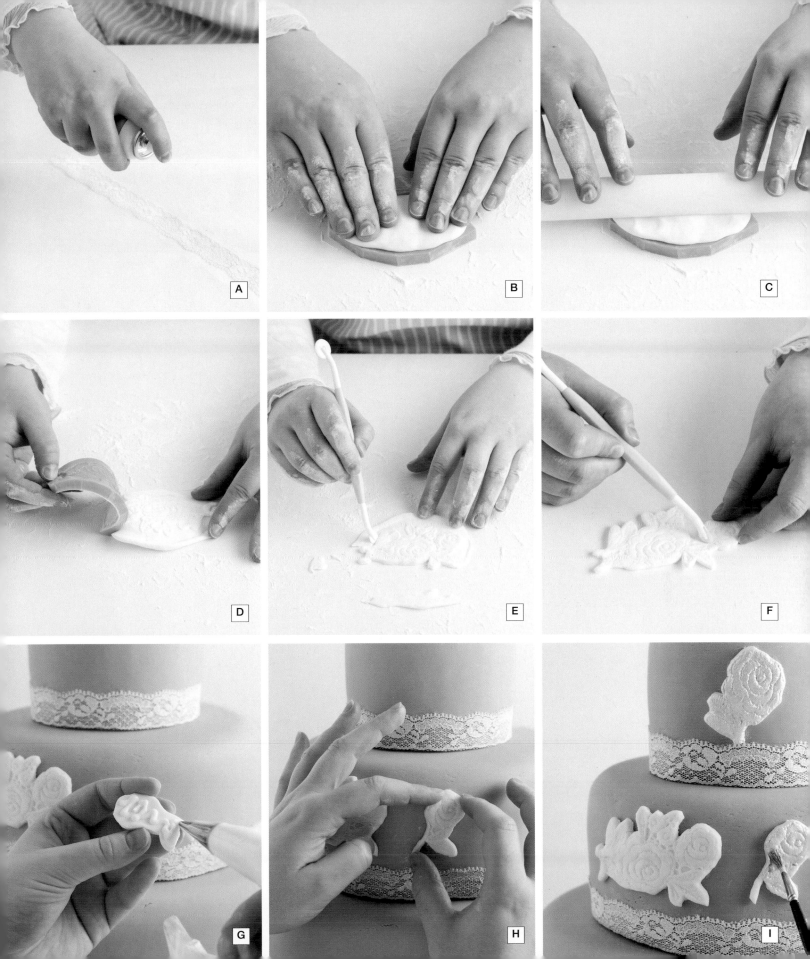

chic and sophisticated

The cakes in this chapter focus on sophistication and luxury with
an added hint of drama. Full of eye-catching centrepieces for
couples unafraid to make a statement, these designs are dedicated
to grandeur and opulence. From striking monochrome designs
to sculptural chocolate creations, 'Chic and Sophisticated' offers
a collection of smart, contemporary and stylish wedding cakes,
perfect for black tie events and glamorous evening receptions.

Royal Ballet

This cake is a real show stopper, with its sculptural chocolate ruffles, reminiscent of a ballerina's tutu. The smell of chocolate will fill the room, enticing the guests to make closer inspection of this impressive design. Royal Ballet is equally stunning in dark or milk chocolate and will make a majestic centrepiece, but please be mindful of the season this cake is to be served in. The delicate chocolate ruffles will not fare well in midsummer heat, and will be trickier to prepare. Whatever time of year you make this cake, keep the kitchen cool and prepare by placing the marble slabs in the freezer a several hours before they are required. I have paired this design with white chocolate and cardamom cake: a sophisticated and playful flavour, which hints at the exotic with its subtle, fragrant spice.

TO MAKE THE WHITE CHOCOLATE AND CARDAMOM CAKE

Following the method below, prepare all 3 tiers of your cake, following the chart on page 146 to determine quantities, pan sizes and cooking times.

1 Preheat the oven to 180°C (160°C fan)/350°F (325°F fan)/Gas 4.

2 Melt the chocolate in a heatproof bowl set over a pan of barely simmering water, then remove from the heat and leave to cool.

3 Smash the cardamom pods open with a pestle and remove the seeds. Discard the shells and place the seeds in the mortar. Grind the seeds to a fine powder and set aside for later.

4 In a large mixing bowl and using an electric whisk, cream together the butter and sugar until pale and fluffy. Gradually add the egg yolks, one at a time, beating well after each addition, then beat in the cooled white chocolate, vanilla extract and ground cardamom seeds.

5 Sift half of the flour over the mixture and beat in, then add the sour cream and beat again to

combine. Sift over the remaining flour and mix again until it is all incorporated.

6 In a separate, spotlessly clean bowl, and with clean beaters, whisk the egg whites with the salt until they form soft peaks.

7 Vigorously beat 1 spoonful of the egg white into the cake batter to help slacken it, then gently fold in the remaining egg white with a metal spoon, being careful not to knock the air out of the mixture.

8 Pour the cake batter into your prepared cake pan, level the top with a palette knife and bake in the preheated oven for 30–40 minutes, or until an inserted skewer comes out clean.

9 Leave the cake to cool in its pan, set on a wire rack, for 10 minutes before turning out onto the rack to cool completely.

10 To make the white chocolate buttercream, whisk together the butter and chocolate, then sift over half the icing/confectioners' sugar and whisk until fully incorporated.

FOR A 15-CM/6-INCH CAKE

75 g/2½ oz. white chocolate, broken into pieces

12–15 green cardamom pods

100 g/6½ tablespoons unsalted butter, softened

100 g/½ cup (caster) sugar

2 medium eggs, separated

½ tablespoon vanilla extract

125 g/1 cup self-raising flour

75 ml/5 tablespoons sour cream

a pinch of salt

FOR THE WHITE CHOCOLATE BUTTERCREAM

100 g/6½ tablespoons unsalted butter, softened

100 g/3½ oz. white chocolate, melted and cooled

200 g/1½ cups icing/confectioners' sugar

½ tablespoon vanilla extract

a splash of milk (optional)

a 15-cm/6-inch deep round cake pan, greased and lined

a thin round cake board the same size as the cake

11 Sift over the remaining icing/confectioners' sugar and whisk until combined, then add the vanilla extract and whisk again. If necessary, add a splash of milk to slacken the mixture, then continue to whisk until pale and creamy. This can take a couple of minutes.

12 Level the cake, if necessary (see page 25), then attach it to the cake board with a small blob of buttercream. Spread the buttercream over the top and sides of the cake with a palette knife (see page 27) and leave to set completely.

tip: for added decadence

This cake is generously iced already, but if you would like to create an even more decadent flavour, you can slice the cakes horizontally in half and fill them with half the white chocolate buttercream before using the rest to cover the tops and sides of the cakes.

TO DECORATE THE CAKE

FOR THE DECORATION

3 cake drums, each 5 cm/ 2 inches larger than the cake that will sit upon it

White Modelling Chocolate (see page 23 for recipe and page 157 for quantities)

1.5-cm/1½-inch wide black satin ribbon

up to 3 kg/6½ lbs. white chocolate for a 15-cm/ 6-inch, 22-cm/9-inch, 30-cm/12-inch cake

2 marble slabs, chilled in the freezer overnight

a chocolate or wallpaper scraper

a small ladle

1 Cover the 3 cake drums with white modelling chocolate, following the instructions on page 26, then set each cake on its own drum and ribbon the cake drums (see page 33).

2 Melt some of the white chocolate in a heatproof bowl set over a pan of barely simmering water. You needn't melt it all at once, it can be done in stages. (You do not need to temper the chocolate for this technique, as the frozen marble will cool the cocoa butter crystals at the same rate and stabilize them.)

3 Remove one of the marble slabs from the freezer (leave the other one in the freezer – you will need to swap them over when the one you are working with gets too warm) and scrape off any excess ice with the scraper.

4 Pour a small ladleful of melted chocolate onto the end of the marble slab furthest away from you. **(A)** Working quickly, scrape the chocolate down the slab, dragging the scraper in a straight line towards your body. **(B)** You should see the chocolate

immediately tighten and start to turn matte as it cools and sets.

5 Use the scraper to gently lift the end of the strip of chocolate, using your other hand to help peel it off the slab. **(C)**

6 Working very quickly, concertina the chocolate with your fingers. **(D)** If the chocolate snaps, it is because you have left it on the frozen slab for too long. If the chocolate becomes too soft to work with, it is most likely due to the temperature of the room you are working in. Open all the windows and try again! If you have a long handle end on your ruffles, you can chop them off using your scraper.

7 Place the finished ruffle on a cool tray or in the fridge to set completely. Repeat until you have enough ruffles for your design.

8 Make a collar for your cakes using the same technique, but, instead of folding the chocolate strip into a concertina to make ruffles, wrap the strip around the cake edge, affixing it to the cake with

a blob of the melted white chocolate. **(E)** Depending on the size of the cake and the length of your marble slab, you may need to make 2 or 3 strips to cover the circumference of the cake. Repeat until the sides of all the cakes are fully collared with chocolate.

9 Start at the outer edges of the cakes and place the ruffles in concentric circles on top, working inwards. **(F)** If you need to, dunk the handle ends of your ruffles in white chocolate to help attach them. Keep layering up the ruffles around the cake to create a beautiful dome on top. **(G)**

Victoriana

FOR A 20-CM/8-INCH CAKE

5 large eggs, separated

¼ teaspoon salt

150 g/¾ cup (caster) sugar

200 g/1 stick plus
5 tablespoons unsalted
butter, melted and cooled

50 g/½ cup ground
almonds

100 g/3½ oz. good quality
(70% cocoa solids) dark
chocolate, melted and
cooled

75 g/⅔ cup self-raising
flour

2 teaspoons baking
powder

50 g/6 tablespoons
unsweetened cocoa
powder

250 g/9 oz. jarred black
cherries soaked in Kirsch,
plus 2 tablespoons Kirsch
from the jar

FOR THE CREAM CHEESE
FROSTING

150 g/1 stick plus
2 tablespoons unsalted
butter, softened

150 g/⅔ cup Philadelphia
cream cheese (see page 4)

600 g/4¼ cups icing/
confectioners' sugar

1 tablespoon vanilla
extract, or to taste

a 20-cm/8-inch deep square
cake pan, greased and
lined

a thin square cake board
the same size as the cake

This stylish cake is simple but grand, with a clean, sharp design. The swags and pearls are reminiscent of Victorian borders and the monochrome colour scheme is smart and sophisticated in its simplicity, and perfect for a formal reception. Black Forest cake is making a comeback thanks to its irresistible combination of chocolate and cherries with a tempting splash of Kirsch. This cake makes a wonderful dessert and is definitely best eaten with a fork.

TO MAKE THE BLACK FOREST CAKE

Following the method below, prepare all 3 tiers of your cake, following the chart on page 147 to determine quantities, pan sizes and cooking times.

1 Preheat the oven to 170°C (150°C fan)/325°F (300°F fan)/Gas 3.

2 In a spotlessly clean bowl, whisk the egg whites with the salt until they form stiff peaks. Set aside.

3 In a large mixing bowl, whisk the egg yolks and sugar to the ribbon stage – pale, thick and mousse-like and the mixture leaves a slowly disappearing trail when you lift the beaters.

4 Whisk in the cooled, melted butter, followed by the ground almonds and melted chocolate, then sift over the flour, baking powder and cocoa powder and fold everything together with a metal spoon.

5 Vigorously beat 1 spoonful of the egg white into the cake batter to help slacken it, then gently fold in the remaining egg white, being careful not to knock the air out of the mixture.

6 Pour the batter into the prepared cake pan and bake in the preheated oven for about 45 minutes or until an inserted skewer comes out clean.

7 Leave the cake to cool in its pan, set on a wire rack, for 10 minutes before turning out onto the rack to cool completely.

8 To make the frosting, whisk together the butter and cream cheese until soft and creamy. Sift over half the icing/confectioners' sugar and whisk until

thoroughly combined, then sift over the remaining sugar and whisk again. Add the vanilla extract and whisk until soft and creamy. Taste for vanilla, adding more if desired.

9 Once cooled, level the cake, if necessary, then slice it horizontally in half using a long, serrated knife (see page 25). Paint the cut side of each cake half with Kirsch, then spread a quarter of the frosting on top of the Kirsch. Arrange a layer of drained cherries on one cake half and top with the remaining cake half, frosting side down.

10 Attach the cake to the cake board with a small blob of the frosting, then cover the top and sides of the cake with the remaining frosting and pop it in the fridge to set completely.

tip: piping black icing

It is best to use disposable plastic piping bags for black royal icing as it is less likely to leak out and dye your hands.

TO DECORATE THE CAKE

FOR THE DECORATION

marzipan (see page 157 for quantities)

white sugar paste (see page 157 for quantities)

a cake drum 8 cm/3 inches larger than the base tier

1.5-cm/¾-inch wide black satin ribbon

1 quantity Royal Icing (see page 20)

black food colouring paste (use extra-black dye for the best results)

a clean ruler

a scribe tool

a black edible ink pen

a piping bag fitted with a fine round nozzle/tip

1 Cover your 3 cake tiers with marzipan (you can brush the cake with more Kirsch to stick on the marzipan if the buttercream is too set) followed by sugar paste, then cover your cake drum in the same white sugar paste (refer to pages 26 and 28–30 for full instructions).

2 Rod and stack the cake (following the instructions on page 32), then ribbon the cake and the cake drum (see page 33).

3 Use the ruler to measure the height of the top tier cake above the ribbon and make a few small marks with a scribe tool to indicate the centre. Repeat this process for all 4 sides of the cake.

4 Using the ruler and edible ink pen, draw a straight horizontal line, linking up the centre marks, so you have a thin guideline around the centre of the entire cake. **(A)** Repeat for the other tiers.

5 Dye the royal icing black with the food colouring paste and spoon it into the piping bag. Applying fairly strong pressure, pipe a row of black pearls, along each guide line. **(B)**

6 Pipe a large pearl above the line at intervals of every seventh pearl.

7 Pipe a smaller pearl, adjoined to it, just above the large pearl. Then another small pearl above, this time with a small gap in between.

8 Using the large pearls as a guide, pipe swags beneath the row of pearls. **(C)**

9 Add details of 2 small pearls on either side of the starting point of each swag, and 2 pearls at the lowest point in the centre of each swag, to mirror the pearls above the row. **(D)**

10 Repeat these steps on each side of every tier of the cake.

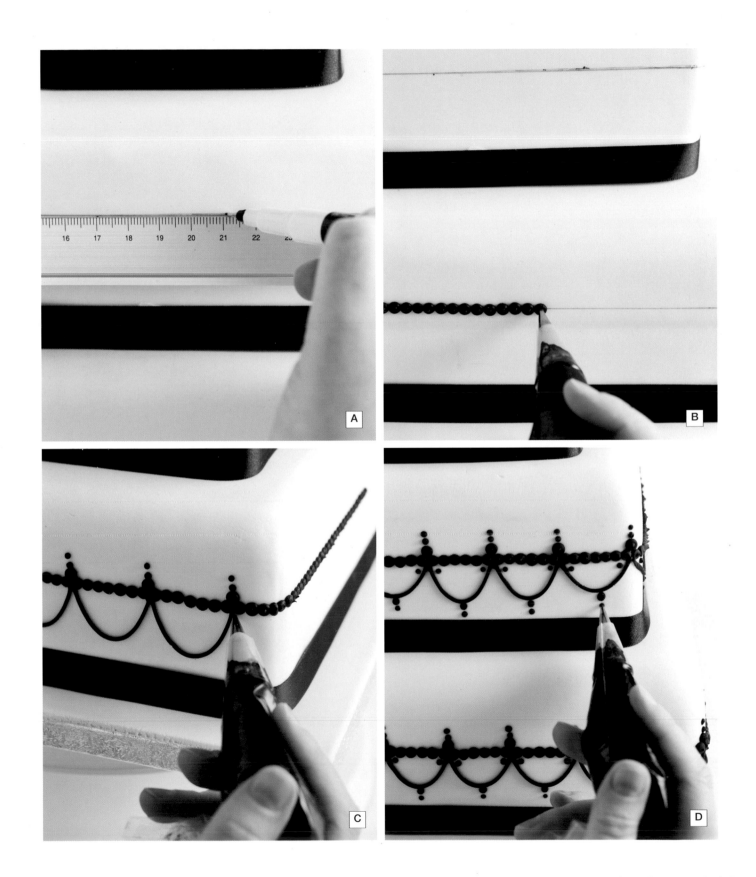

Film Noir

These black and white miniatures are perfect for an intimate cocktail reception. Their smart monochrome design is inspired by the film noir genre, and two of its most stylish stars, Lauren Bacall and Humphrey Bogart. Chocolate and Guinness cake is a decadently dark chocolate cake. The Guinness adds an extra layer of flavour, giving the cake an almost smoky, spicy depth. This recipe makes seven individual cakes. Divide your number of guests by seven to work out batch quantities if serving as dessert. For coffee-sized portions, divide your number of guests by 14, as each individual cake can be cut in half to feed two people.

TO MAKE THE CHOCOLATE AND GUINNESS CAKES

Following the method below, prepare as many batches of cakes as required in multiples of 7.

1 Preheat the oven to 180°C (160°C fan)/350°F (325°F fan)/Gas 4.

2 Melt the chocolate in a heatproof bowl set over a pan of barely simmering water, then remove from the heat and leave to cool.

3 In a large mixing bowl and using an electric whisk, cream together the butter and sugar until pale and fluffy, before gradually beating in the eggs.

4 Whisk the Guinness into the melted chocolate and decant into a jug/pitcher.

5 Sift together the flour, baking powder, bicarbonate of soda/baking soda, cocoa powder and salt, then whisk a third of this dry mixture into the butter and sugar. Pour in a third of the Guinness mixture and whisk through. Continue to add thirds of the dry and wet ingredients alternately, mixing well between each addition, until everything is combined.

6 Pour the batter into your prepared roulade tray/jelly roll pan and bake in the preheated oven for 20–30 minutes, or until an inserted skewer comes out clean.

7 Leave the cake to cool in its pan, set on a wire rack, for 10 minutes before turning out onto the rack to cool completely.

8 To make the vanilla mascarpone frosting, beat the butter until very soft and fluffy. Gradually stir in the mascarpone. Do not use an electric whisk! If you do, the mascarpone will become too runny to work with.

9 Sift over the icing/confectioners' sugar in stages, stirring it into the butter and mascarpone with a fork between each addition. Once all the icing/confectioners' sugar has been incorporated, add the vanilla and mix thoroughly. Taste for vanilla, adding more if necessary.

10 Referring to the full instructions on page 31, stamp out 14 discs from the sponge with the cutter. Stack and cover 7 pairs of sponge discs with the frosting, affixing each to a thin cake board. Cover half the cakes with white sugar paste and the other half with black.

FOR 7 SMALL CAKES

150 g/5½ oz. good quality (70% cocoa solids) dark chocolate, broken into pieces

170 g/1½ sticks unsalted butter, softened

260 g/1⅓ cups dark muscovado sugar

3 large eggs, beaten

330 ml/11 oz. Guinness

170 g/1⅓ cups plain/all-purpose flour

¾ teaspoon baking powder

1½ teaspoons bicarbonate of soda/baking soda

150 g/1 cup plus 3 tablespoons unsweetened cocoa powder

¼ teaspoon salt

black and white sugar pastes (see page 157 for quantities)

FOR THE VANILLA MASCARPONE FROSTING

115 g/1 stick unsalted butter, softened

115 g/½ cup mascarpone cheese

175 g/1½ cups icing/confectioners' sugar

2 teaspoons vanilla extract, or to taste

a 23 x 33-cm/9 x 13-inch roulade tray/jelly roll pan, greased and lined

an 8-cm/3-inch round pastry cutter

7 x 8-cm/3-inch thin round cake boards

FOR THE DECORATION

1.5-cm/¾-inch wide white satin ribbon

1.5-cm/¾-inch wide black satin ribbon

white and black floristry pastes (approx. 15–20 g/½ oz. for the flower petals and 4–5 g/⅛ oz. for the centres)

cornflour/cornstarch, for dusting

sunflower or vegetable oil

1 quantity Royal Icing (see page 20)

extra-black food colouring paste

3.5-cm/1¼-inch and 5-cm/2-inch 5-petal blossom cutters

a foam modelling mat

a ball tool

a folding flower stand

a daisy centre mould

2 piping bags fitted with medium–fine nozzles/tips

TO DECORATE THE CAKES

1 Ribbon each small cake, using white ribbon for the black cakes and black ribbon for the white cakes (see page 33).

2 Knead a small ball of white floristry paste until pliable, then roll it out very thinly on a cornflour/cornstarch-dusted surface (it is important to only use small pieces of floristry paste at a time, as it dries out very quickly). Use the blossom cutters to stamp out 1 large and 1 small blossom for each of the black cakes. **(A)**

3 Place the blossoms on a foam modelling mat and, using a ball tool, roll out the edges of the petals **(B)**, then lay them in a folding flower stand so that the flowers will dry in a good shape. Press into the centre of each blossom with the ball tool to create a hollow for the centre of the flower to sit in. **(C)**

4 Repeat steps 2–3 using black floristry paste, until you have enough small and large blossoms to create flowers for the white cakes.

5 Next, create the centres for the flowers. Brush the inside of the daisy centre mould with a tiny amount of oil and press a small ball of kneaded white floristry paste into the mould before turning out and leaving to dry. Repeat until you have enough white centres for the black flowers, re-oiling the mould occasionally. In the same way, make flower centres using the black floristry paste, washing and drying the mould first. **(D)**

6 Spoon half of the royal icing into one of the piping bags. Tint the remaining icing jet black with the dye, then spoon it into the other piping bag. Pipe a blob of white icing on top of a black cake, lay a large white blossom in the centre, and press down with the ball tool to firmly secure it. **(E)**

7 Pipe a second blob of icing into the centre of the large flower **(F)** and place the small flower on top, pressing down again with the ball tool. **(G)**

8 Pipe a little icing onto the back of a black flower centre and push it gently into the centre of the double-petalled flower. **(H)**

9 Repeat steps 6–8 to decorate the remaining black cakes, then repeat the same steps for the white cakes, reversing the colours.

10 To finish, pipe the sides of the cakes with vertical, evenly spaced lines of 7 pearls – black pearls on white cakes and white pearls on black cakes. **(I)**

Midnight Lotus

FOR A 20-CM/8-INCH CAKE

8 large eggs, separated, plus 2 whole eggs

¼ teaspoon salt

400 g/2 cups packed dark muscovado sugar

250 g/2½ cups ground almonds

400 g/14 oz. good quality (70% cocoa solids) dark chocolate, melted and cooled

1½ tablespoons dark rum

FOR THE WHIPPED RUM GANACHE

150 g/5½ oz. good quality (70% cocoa solids) dark chocolate, broken into pieces

150 ml/⅔ cup single/ light cream

¼ teaspoon salt

75 g/5 tablespoons unsalted butter, softened

100 g/¾ cup icing/ confectioners' sugar

3 tablespoons dark rum, or to taste

2 x 20-cm/8-inch shallow square cake pans, greased and lined

a thin square cake board the same size as the cake

This striking design is the embodiment of luxury and indulgence. The stunning gold leaf and white chocolate lotus flowers create a mood of mystery and exoticism, redolent of Indian summer nights. A sumptuous and opulent cake deserves a seductive flavour to go with it. I have paired this design with chocolate rum truffle cake: a rich, close-textured chocolate cake laced with rum and filled with satin smooth whipped chocolate ganache. This gluten-free cake is the perfect end to any wedding breakfast and can be adapted to include an alternative favourite spirit or liqueur – brandy, whisky, Cointreau and Amaretto all make delicious options.

TO MAKE THE CHOCOLATE RUM TRUFFLE CAKE

Following the method below, prepare all 3 tiers of your cake, following the chart on page 148 to determine quantities, pan sizes and cooking times.

1 Preheat the oven to 170°C (150°C fan)/325°F (300°F fan)/Gas 3.

2 In a large, spotlessly clean bowl, whisk the egg whites with the salt until they form stiff peaks. Set aside until needed.

3 In a large mixing bowl, whisk together the egg yolks, whole eggs and sugar to the ribbon stage – the mixture should be pale and mousse-like and leave a slowly disappearing ribbon on the surface of the mixture when the excess drips into the bowl from the beaters. This process will take a good few minutes with an electric whisk, so be patient.

4 Fold in the ground almonds, followed by the melted and cooled chocolate, being careful not to knock out any air from the mixture.

5 Finally, with a large metal spoon, fold the beaten egg whites into the batter. Be firm but gentle and don't over-mix the batter or you'll knock out the air in the cake – vital for both the correct texture and also the height of the cakes.

6 Pour the batter into your prepared cake pans and pop them in the preheated oven to bake for about 30–35 minutes, or until an inserted skewer comes out clean.

7 Once baked, place the warm cakes, still in their pans, on a wire rack and stab them all over with a skewer. Drizzle the dark rum over the cakes, then leave to cool in the pans before turning out.

8 To make the whipped rum ganache, put the chocolate in a heatproof bowl and pour the cream into a small saucepan set over a gentle heat. Once the cream scalds, pour it over the chocolate and leave for a minute before stirring in with a rubber spatula until all the chocolate has melted. Stir in the salt, then leave to cool.

9 Whisk the butter until soft, then sift over half of the icing/confectioners' sugar and whisk again until well combined. Sift over the remaining icing/confectioners' sugar and again, whisk thoroughly, then add the rum and whisk a final time.

10 Pour the cooled chocolate mixture over the rum buttercream and whisk until well combined. Taste for rum, adding a little more if you want to, but not too much, or the filling may not set properly. Pop the filling in the fridge for an hour to set, but whisk it again before using.

11 Level the cakes, if necessary (see page 25), then attach one of the cakes to the cake board with a small blob of ganache. Sandwich the cakes together with half of the ganache, then spread the remaining ganache over the top and sides of the cake with a palette knife (see page 27) and leave to set.

FOR THE DECORATION

Dark Modelling Chocolate (see page 23 for recipe and page 157 for quantities), plus a little extra for the lotus bases

a splash of dark rum

a cake drum 8 cm/3 inches larger than the base tier

1.5-cm/¾-inch wide chocolate-brown satin ribbon

approx. 300 g/10½ oz. White Modelling Chocolate (see page 23)

icing/confectioners' sugar, for dusting

1 quantity Royal Icing (see page 20)

clear alcohol (such as vodka)

5–10 x 8-cm/3-inch square sheets of edible gold leaf

small, medium and large calyx cutters

a ball tool

a folding flower tray

an 8-cm/3-inch 5-pointed star cutter

a foam flower former

a piping bag fitted with a small round nozzle

a paintbrush

a clean, dry brush

1 Cover your 3 cake tiers and the cake drum with modelling chocolate, brushing the cakes with a little dark rum first to help it stick (modelling chocolate can be used to cover cakes in the same way as sugar paste – refer to pages 26 and 28–30 for full instructions).

2 Rod and stack the cake (following the instructions on page 32), then ribbon the cake and the cake drum (see page 33).

3 To make a large lotus flower for the top of the cake, knead a piece of white modelling chocolate until pliable and roll it out on a surface dusted with icing/confectioners' sugar. Stamp out 2 calyxs from each size cutter. Use a ball tool to roll from the centre of each calyx out to the edge, to shape the petals and make them more delicate. Use your finger and thumb to pinch the ends to keep the lotus petals pointed. **(A)**

4 Place the 6 calyxs in the small holes of a folding flower tray. Using a ball tool, gently press in the centre of 1 large, 1 medium and 1 small calyx to raise their petals, so they set fairly upright. **(B)** Leave the remaining 3 calyxs to set as they are, so their petal edges set at a lower angle.

5 Using the star cutter, stamp out 2 stars from the rolled-out white chocolate. **(C)** With the ball tool, roll from their centres out, ensuring, again, that the tips of the stars remain pointed. Leave them in a foam flower former to set. **(D)**

6 Repeat steps 3–5 twice more, so you have petals for 3 large lotus flowers for the top of the cake.

7 For a small flower for the side of the cake, follow step 3, but cut out 3 medium and 3 small calyxs. Place them in the folding flower tray and use the ball tool to shape them so that the petals of each size calyx dry at 3 slightly different angles, which will allow them to be stacked.

8 Repeating step 7, prepare enough calyxs for 7–8 small flowers for the sides of the cake. (You could also make a few extra in case any petals break off as you are assembling the flowers!)

9 Once all the petal pieces have set, you can start to stack them to create the flowers. Spoon the royal icing into the piping bag.

E

F

G

H

I

J

10 For a large flower, take one of the stars from the flower former and pipe a blob of icing in the centre **(E)**, then set a second star on top so that the points fall between those of the first. Continue to stack the flower, adding the calyxs in descending size order, with the calyx with the less-upright petals first **(F)**, affixing each one with a blob of icing. **(G)** When the last calyx has been added, press down in the centre of the flower with a ball tool to ensure they are firmly secured **(H)**, then leave to set. Repeat for the remaining large flowers.

11 Repeat step 10 to make the small flowers, starting with the medium calyx with the least-

upright petals first. When all the petals are stacked, press down with a ball tool to secure firmly. Repeat until you have constructed all of the lotus flowers. **(I)**

12 Next, gild the cake. Before you start, close the windows and/or turn off any fans as you need a still atmosphere to create the best results. Using the paintbrush dipped in alcohol, gently dampen the area of the cake you want to gild. **(J)**

13 Place the sheet of gold leaf on the dampened area and gently press it down with a clean, dry brush. Peel off the rest of the sheet and you should be left with a piece of golf leaf, distressed at the

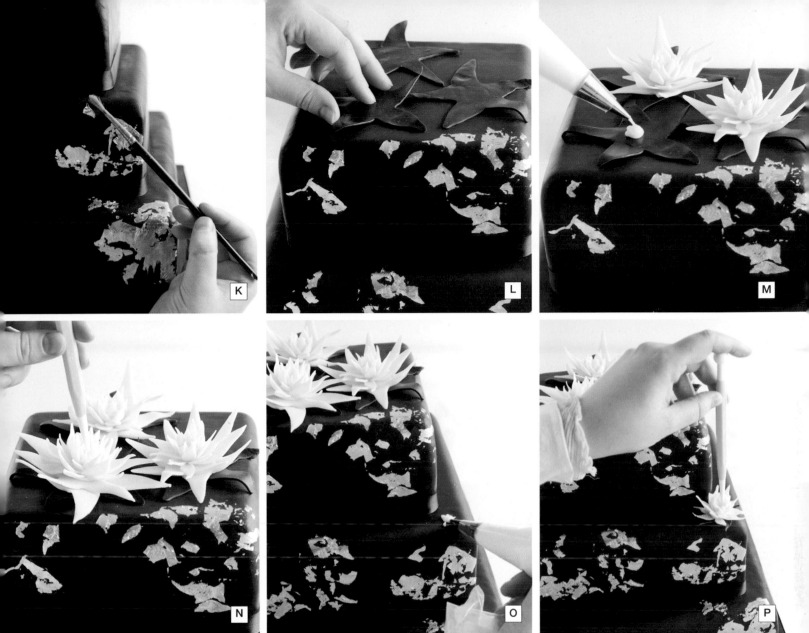

edges. For a more distressed look, use the dry brush to rub away small areas of the gold leaf. **(K)** Continue adding gold leaf to the cake, until you have covered as much of the cake as you wish.

14 Make the bases the flowers will sit on just before you affix them to the cake, so they are still pliable. Knead and roll out a small amount of dark modelling chocolate and stamp out 3 stars with the star cutter and 7–8 large calyxs. Using the ball tool, as before, roll out the star and calyx points to make them finer.

15 Attach the 3 dark chocolate star flower bases to the top of the cake using a blob of royal icing. Gently

shape the points, curling and bending them slightly, to achieve attractive natural 'leaf' bases (which don't sit completely flat) **(L)**, then leave them to set.

16 Attach your large lotus flowers on top of the bases with more royal icing **(M)**, pressing down in the centre of each flower with a ball tool to make sure they are firmly secured. **(N)** Repeat the process for the small lotus flowers on the corner edges of the cake **(O)**, using the dark chocolate bases cut with the calyx cutter. Add a small lotus flower onto each base with a little royal icing, press down with a ball tool **(P)**, then leave the cake in a cool place to set.

chic and sophisticated **83**

Art Nouveau

Inspired by the work of Aubrey Beardsley, this Art Nouveau-style design makes a real statement. Its elegant lines and striking monochrome colour scheme create a strong sense of drama, perfect for black tie weddings and evening receptions. Espresso génoise cake is the perfect accompaniment to this design, with its dark, sophisticated and stylish charm. This cake looks beautiful as it is or topped with fresh flowers. I love the vibrancy of deep red roses, but you can choose any flowers you like, as long as you ensure they're not poisonous.

FOR A 23-CM/9-INCH CAKE

375 g/1¾ cups (caster) sugar

12 large eggs

75 g/5 tablespoons unsalted butter, melted

2 teaspoons instant espresso powder dissolved in 1½ tablespoons hot water

375 g/3 cups plain/all-purpose flour

FOR THE ESPRESSO BUTTERCREAM

150 g/1 stick plus 2 tablespoons unsalted butter, softened

300 g/2 cups plus 2 tablespoons icing/confectioners' sugar

2 teaspoons instant espresso powder dissolved in 1½ tablespoons hot water

a splash of milk (optional)

a 23-cm/9-inch deep round cake pan, greased and lined

a thin round cake board the same size as the cake

TO MAKE THE ESPRESSO CAKE

Following the method below, prepare all 3 tiers of your cake, following the chart on page 141 to determine quantities, pan sizes and cooking times.

1 Preheat the oven to 180°C (160°C fan)/350°F (325°F fan)/Gas 4.

2 Put the sugar and eggs in a large heatproof bowl set over a pan of gently simmering water. Use an electric whisk to beat continuously until the mixture is hot. Carefully remove the bowl from the heat and continue to whisk on high speed for 10 minutes. The mixture should double in volume and be at the ribbon stage – pale, thick and mousse-like and leave a slowly disappearing trail when you lift the beaters.

3 Whisk the melted butter into the egg mixture, followed by the prepared espresso.

4 Sift the flour onto the mixture and fold in using a large metal spoon, being careful not to overmix and knock the air out of the batter.

5 Pour the batter into your prepared cake pan and bake in the preheated oven for 30–35 minutes, or until an inserted skewer comes out clean.

6 Leave the cake to cool completely in its pan, set on a wire rack, before turning out.

7 While the cake is cooling, make the espresso buttercream. In a large mixing bowl, whisk the butter until very soft using an electric whisk. Sift over half the icing/confectioners' sugar and whisk until thoroughly combined, then sift over the remaining icing/confectioners' sugar and continue to whisk until all the sugar is incorporated. Add the prepared espresso and continue to whisk. If the buttercream seems too firm, you can add a splash of milk at this stage to slacken the mixture. Continue to whisk on full speed until very soft and spreadable.

8 Once cool, level the cake, if necessary, then slice it horizontally in half using a long, serrated knife (see page 25). Sandwich the cake halves with half of the buttercream. Attach the cake to the cake board with a small blob of buttercream, then spread the remaining buttercream over the top and sides of the cake with a palette knife (see page 27).

TO DECORATE THE CAKE

FOR THE DECORATION

marzipan (see page 157 for quantities)

white sugar paste (see page 157 for quantities)

a cake drum 8 cm/3 inches larger than the base tier

1.5-cm/¾-inch black satin ribbon

½ quantity Royal Icing (see page 20)

extra-black food colouring paste

a scribe tool

a piping bag fitted with a very fine nozzle/tip

a piping bag fitted with a fine nozzle/tip

a soft brush

1 Cover your 3 cake tiers with marzipan, followed by sugarpaste, then cover your cake drum in the same white sugar paste (refer to pages 26 and 28–30 for full instructions).

2 Rod and stack the cake (following the instructions on page 32), then ribbon the cake and the cake drum (see page 33).

3 Trace the patterns below onto separate squares of baking parchment. (The confident amongst you can pipe the design around the cake free-hand, but be aware that once the icing touches the cake, mistakes cannot be scraped off – black dye will leave an untidy and permanent mark. But fear not, you can always turn mistakes into beautiful embellishments with a little creative ingenuity!)

4 Once traced, hold the baking parchment stencil against the cake and prick along the lines of the pattern with a scribe tool **(A)**, so that once you remove the parchment you have a guide to join the dots. You can copy the picture of my finished cake or you can build your patterns in any way you wish to make the design your own. Make sure you have built up the pattern over the whole cake with the scribe tool before you start piping, or you may smudge the black icing with your stencil.

5 Dye the royal icing black with the food colouring paste and divide it between the 2 piping bags. Use the piping bag fitted with the very fine nozzle/tip for the petals and stems, and simply follow the dots to build up pattern. You will need to pressure pipe the more intricate shapes of the petals; make contact with the cake surface then apply even pressure on the bag with your thumb as you gently guide the nozzle/tip along the dotted line, keeping it at an angle. **(B)**

6 Once the stems and petals are piped, go back and pipe on the leaves. **(C)**

7 Swap to the piping bag fitted with the fine nozzle/tip to create the stamen of the lilies and the central dots of the daisies **(D)**, then leave the icing to set.

TEMPLATES

a splash of colour

Delicate, fun and pretty, the wedding cakes in this chapter are
a celebration of feminine warmth and charm. Enchanting and
enticing, these cakes have a lovely vintage feel and are paired
with light, friendly flavours, perfect for relaxed occasions.
A design from this chapter would be the ideal choice for sunny
days in bunting-filled gardens and warm evenings lit by paper
lanterns. Delightful and fresh, these cakes are perfect for
laid-back, colourful and romantic weddings.

Something Borrowed...

These delightful miniature cakes are perfect for intimate weddings. The pretty white butterflies on Wedgwood blue icing will create a fresh, crisp centrepiece at any reception. This delicate decoration is exquisite partnered with pistachio and orange blossom cake. The fragrant, light sponge is moist and delicious, perfect as a summery dessert or a tempting treat later in the evening with coffee. The miniature cakes provide a perfect portion for one. The recipe makes enough for either a top tier or eight individual cakes. You can work out the number of batches you will need to make for miniatures, by dividing your number of guests by eight.

TO MAKE THE PISTACHIO AND ORANGE BLOSSOM CAKES

Following the method below, prepare as many batches of miniature cakes as required, in multiples of 8, plus a top tier cake for cutting.

1 Preheat the oven to 180°C (160°C fan)/350°F (325°F fan)/Gas 4.

2 In a large mixing bowl and using an electric whisk, whisk the whole eggs and the icing/confectioners' sugar together until pale and fluffy. Add the ground pistachios and continue whisking on high speed for about 6 minutes, then add the melted butter and flour and stir in until thoroughly incorporated.

3 In a separate, spotlessly clean bowl, whisk the eggs whites with the salt until they form soft peaks, then whisk in the caster/superfine sugar in 2 stages and continue whisking until the meringue is stiff and glossy.

4 Vigorously beat a third of the meringue into the cake batter to help slacken it, then gently fold in the remaining meringue, being careful not to knock the air out of the mixture.

5 Pour the batter into your prepared roulade tray/jelly roll pan or shallow cake pans and use a palette knife to smooth it out. Bake in the preheated oven for 10–15 minutes for the roulade tray/jelly roll pan or 15–20 minutes for the cake pans, or until the sponge is no longer sticky to the touch.

6 Leave the cake to cool in its tray or pan, set on a wire rack, for 10 minutes before turning out onto the rack to cool completely.

7 For the orange blossom icing, whisk together the butter and cream cheese with an electric whisk. Sift over half the icing/confectioners' sugar and whisk until fully combined, then sift over the remaining icing/confectioners' sugar and whisk again until soft and creamy. Whisk in the orange blossom water, taste and add more if needed.

8 For the miniature cakes, referring to the full instructions on page 31, stamp out 24 discs from the sponge with the cutter. Stack and cover 8 sets of 3 sponge discs with the icing, affixing each to a thin cake board.

For the top tier, level the cakes, if necessary (see page 25), then attach one of the cakes to the cake board with a small blob of icing. Sandwich the cakes together with half of the icing, then spread the remaining icing over the top and sides of the cake with a palette knife (see page 27) and leave to set.

FOR 8 MINIATURE CAKES OR A 15-CM/6-INCH TOP TIER CUTTING CAKE

3 large eggs, plus 5 egg whites

175 g/1½ cups icing/ confectioners' sugar, sifted

175 g/1¼ cups ground pistachio nuts

40 g/3 tablespoons unsalted butter, melted

50 g/6 tablespoons plain/all-purpose flour, sifted

a pinch of salt

50 g/¼ cup caster/ superfine sugar

FOR THE ORANGE BLOSSOM ICING

50 g/3 tablespoons plus 1 teaspoon unsalted butter, softened

50 g/3 tablespoons Philadelphia cream cheese (see page 4)

200 g/1⅔ cups icing/ confectioners' sugar

1 tablespoon orange blossom water, or to taste

a 23 x 33-cm/9 x 13-inch roulade tray/jelly roll pan, greased and lined
OR
2 x 15-cm/6-inch shallow round cake pans, greased and lined

a 5-cm/2-inch round cutter

8 x 5-cm/2-inch thin round cake boards
OR
a thin 15-cm/6-inch round cake board

FOR THE DECORATION

550 g/1 lb. 4 oz. marzipan

Wedgwood blue sugar paste (see the tip below for achieving this colour and page 157 for quantities)

a cake drum 5 cm/2 inches larger than the top tier

1 quantity Royal Icing (see page 20)

1.5-cm/½-inch wide white satin ribbon

white floristry paste (approx. 8 g/¼ oz. for a large butterfly and 4 g/⅛ oz. for a small one)

cornflour/cornstarch, for dusting

large and small butterfly cutters

a wheel tool

a piece of strong card, folded

a piping bag fitted with a very fine round nozzle/tip

TO DECORATE THE CAKES

1 Cover the top tier cake with marzipan followed by sugarpaste, then cover your cake drum in the same Wedgwood blue sugar paste (refer to pages 26 and 28–30 for full instructions). Smooth a generous blob of royal icing over the centre of the iced cake drum and set the top tier cake onto it.

2 Cover each of the miniature cakes with sugar paste (referring, again, to page 31 for full instructions).

3 Ribbon each miniature cake, the top tier and the cake drum with the white ribbon (see page 33).

4 Knead a ball of white floristry paste until pliable, then roll it out very thinly on a cornflour/cornstarch-dusted surface. (It is important to use only small pieces of floristry paste at a time, as it dries out very quickly.) Use the cutters to stamp out 1 or 2 large butterflies **(A)** as well as several small ones for the top tier, then cut out a small butterfly for each miniature cake. **(B)**

5 Using the wheel tool, make an impression on either side of the body of the butterfly, being careful not to cut deep enough to detach the wings. **(C)**

6 Place the butterflies inside the folded card, so their wings dry at an angle. Hold either side of the card in place with a couple of glasses or similar. **(D)** Leave the butterflies to dry overnight in the card.

tip: Wedgwood blue

The beautiful colour of these cakes is inspired by the famous British pottery company, Wedgwood, whose stunning blue designs finished with white detail are synonymous with this pretty colour. To recreate it in sugar paste, use baby blue food colouring paste, cut through with a touch of violet.

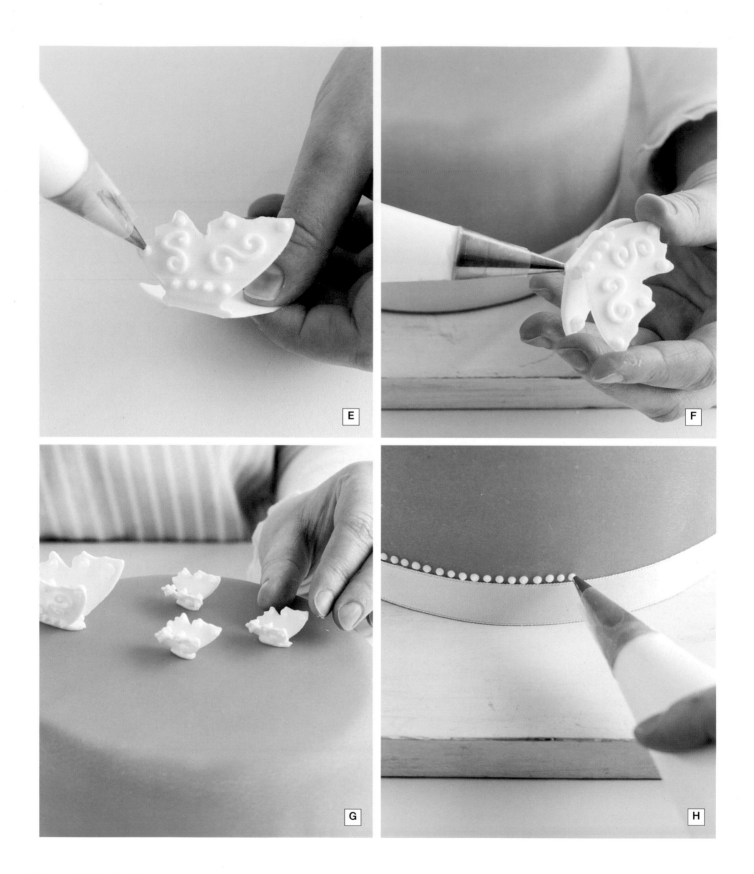

7 Spoon the royal icing into the piping bag and pipe details onto the wings and bodies of the butterflies to decorate **(E)** – be very gentle as the butterflies will break easily. Leave them to set.

8 When set, pipe royal icing along the underside of the body of each butterfly **(F)** and attach 1 or 2 large and several small butterflies to the top of the top tier cake. **(G)** Attach a small butterfly to the top of each miniature cake in the same way.

9 Using the same piping bag, pipe a line of small dots around each cake, just above the ribbon. **(H)**

10 Finally, create triangulated patterns of small dots around the butterflies and in a diagonal stripe down the sides of the miniature cakes.

Vintage Rose

FOR 12 CUPCAKES

100 g/6½ tablespoons
unsalted butter, softened

100 g/½ cup (caster) sugar

2 large eggs

100 g/¾ cup self-raising
flour, sifted

½ teaspoon baking
powder

2 teaspoons vanilla
extract, or to taste

a splash of milk (optional)

FOR THE VANILLA
BUTTERCREAM

75 g/5 tablespoons
unsalted butter, softened

150 g/1 cup icing/
confectioners' sugar

2 teaspoons vanilla
extract, or to taste

a splash of milk (optional)

*a 12-hole muffin pan, lined
with paper cupcake cases*

These simple, pretty cupcakes are friendly and inviting. With their vintage-style sugar roses, these homely treats are reminiscent of Cath Kidston's iconic floral designs. Vintage Rose is the perfect design for informal, shabby chic and garden weddings. Popular with everyone, young and old, I have paired this design with classic and delicious vanilla cupcakes. Comforting and cheering, vanilla cake topped with vanilla buttercream is the perfect flavour for these charmingly nostalgic and softly feminine cakes.

TO MAKE THE VANILLA CUPCAKES

Following the method below, prepare as many batches of cupcakes as required, using the chart on page 150 to determine larger batch quantities.

1 Preheat the oven to 180°C (160°C fan)/350°F (325°F fan)/Gas 4.

2 In a large mixing bowl and using an electric whisk, beat together the butter, sugar, eggs, flour and baking powder for a few minutes, until the batter is pale and fluffy. Add the vanilla extract, beat in, then taste the batter, adding more vanilla if desired. Slacken the mixture with a splash of milk, if necessary

3 Fill your cupcake cases two thirds of the way up with cake batter and bake in the preheated oven for 15–20 minutes, or until a skewer inserted into one of the cakes comes out clean.

4 Leave the cakes to cool in the pan for 10 minutes before lifting them out and transferring them to a wire rack to cool completely.

5 To make the buttercream, whisk the butter with an electric whisk until really soft and fluffy. Sift half the icing/confectioners' sugar over the butter and whisk until thoroughly combined, then sift over the remaining icing/confectioners' sugar and whisk again until all incorporated. Whisk in the vanilla extract, then taste the buttercream, adding more vanilla if desired. Slacken the mixture with a splash of milk, if necessary, then proceed directly to the decorating steps overleaf.

tip: for a vanilla tier

You can adapt this design to include a top tier by following the instructions for crumb-coating and covering a large cake in buttercream (see page 27) and creating larger roses like those found on the Brighton Rock cake (see pages 108–109). Alternatively, if you would like to include a classic, vanilla-flavoured tier in any of the other designs found in the book, you can find the ingredients quantities and baking times on page 150.

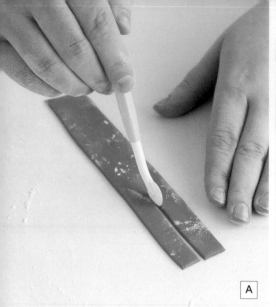

A

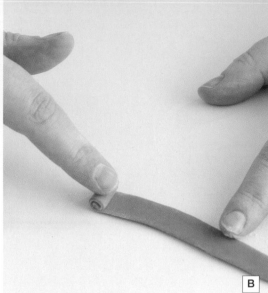

B

C

FOR THE DECORATION

hot pink sugar paste (approx. 10 g/¼ oz. per 3 roses)

grass green sugar paste (approx. 3 g/¹⁄₁₆ oz. per 3 leaves)

icing/confectioners' sugar, for dusting

clear alcohol (such as vodka) or cooled boiled water

a wheel tool
a small paintbrush
a small step palette knife

TO DECORATE THE CAKES

1 Knead and roll out a piece of pink sugar paste on a flat surface lightly dusted with icing/confectioners' sugar. Cut into strips about 1 cm/½ inch thick using the wheel tool. **(A)**

2 Roll up each strip to create a rose shape, using your index finger to gently nudge the roll forwards. **(B)**

3 Once you have the desired rose thickness, slice off the end of the strip with a wheel tool **(C)** and roll up the excess. **(D)**

4 Repeat this process until you have made enough roses for 3 per cupcake. **(E)**

D

E

F

5 To make the leaves, knead a piece of the green sugar paste until pliable, before pinching off a tiny piece. Drag it away from the ball of sugar paste so that a natural point forms **(F)**, then tidy it into a leaf shape using your index finger and thumb. **(G)**

6 Attach a leaf to each rose by dampening the bottom of the rose slightly with a paintbrush dipped in clear alcohol or cooled boiled water, and sticking a leaf to the moistened area with the tip of the leaf pointing outwards. **(H)**

7 Smooth the prepared buttercream over the tops of the cupcakes using a small step palette knife. **(I)** Make sure you spread the buttercream right to the edges of the paper cases to prevent the cakes from drying out.

8 Use the roses to top the cupcakes (the buttercream will be enough for them to stick), 3 to each cake, with the leaves pointing outwards. **(J)**

Love Birds

This rustic, pretty wedding cake will make a beautiful focal point for a shabby chic reception. The gilded birdcages against the soft, sage green icing with accents of pink, create an enchanting, vintage feel, perfect for a country garden wedding. The charming pair of lovebirds perching on a golden branch with tenderly touching beaks, complete the romantic picture. I have matched this design with a lightly spiced and zesty carrot cake with a deliciously creamy lemon filling. I have added pecans and orange-soaked sultanas, but you can substitute them with walnuts and raisins or leave them out altogether if you would prefer. This cake looks beautiful topped with pink flowers; a hydrangea head or pink peonies are both lovely options

TO MAKE THE CARROT CAKE

Following the method below, prepare all 3 tiers of your cake, following the chart on page 151 to determine quantities, pan sizes and cooking times.

1 Preheat the oven to 150°C (135°C fan)/ 300°F (275°F fan)/Gas 2.

2 Soak the sultanas/golden raisins in the orange juice for at least half an hour, until plumped up, then drain and set aside.

3 In a large mixing bowl and using an electric whisk, beat together the eggs, sunflower oil and muscovado sugar until completely combined and slightly frothy.

4 Add the grated carrot, chopped pecans (if using) and drained sultanas/golden raisins, then stir together with a spoon. Sift the dry ingredients over the mixture and stir to combine, then fold in the orange zest.

5 Divide the batter equally between the prepared cake pans and bake in the preheated oven for

35–40 minutes, or until an inserted skewer comes out clean.

6 Leave the cakes to cool in their pans, set on a wire rack, for 10 minutes before turning out onto the rack to cool completely.

7 For the cream cheese icing, whisk together the cream cheese, butter and half the lemon juice until smooth. Sift over half the icing/confectioners' sugar and whisk, then sift over the remaining icing/ confectioners' sugar and whisk again until creamy. Taste the icing for lemon, whisking in a little more juice if desired.

8 Level the cakes, if necessary (see page 25), then attach one of the cakes to the cake board with a small blob of icing. Sandwich the cakes together with half of the icing, then spread the remaining icing over the top and sides of the cake with a palette knife (see page 27) and leave to set.

FOR A 15-CM/6-INCH CAKE

75 g/½ cup sultanas/ golden raisins

finely grated zest and freshly squeezed juice of 1 large orange

2 large eggs, beaten

150 ml/⅔ cup sunflower oil

200 g/1 cup packed light muscovado sugar

250 g/1¼ cups grated carrot

75 g/¾ cup pecan nuts, roughly chopped (optional)

175 g/1⅓ cups self-raising flour

1 teaspoon bicarbonate of soda/baking soda

½ teaspoon grated nutmeg

2 teaspoons ground cinnamon

1 teaspoon mixed/ apple-pie spice

a pinch of salt

FOR THE LEMON CREAM CHEESE ICING

125 g/½ cup Philadelphia cream cheese (see page 4)

75 g/5 tablespoons unsalted butter, softened

freshly squeezed juice of 1 lemon

300 g/2 cups plus 2 tablespoons icing/ confectioners' sugar

2 x 15-cm/6-inch shallow round cake pans, greased and lined

a thin round cake board the same size as the cake

TO DECORATE THE CAKE

FOR THE DECORATION

marzipan (see page 157
for quantities)

sage green sugar paste
(see page 157 for
quantities)

a cake drum 8 cm/3 inches
larger than the base tier

1.5-cm/½-inch wide gold
ribbon

1.5-cm/½–¾-inch wide
pink organza ribbon

1-cm/⅜-inch wide white
satin ribbon

1 quantity Royal Icing
(see page 20)

antique gold edible
lustre dust

rejuvenator fluid

clear alcohol (such as
vodka) or cooled, boiled
water

approx. 30 g/1 oz. white
floristry paste

icing/confectioners'
sugar, for dusting

approx. 175 g/6 oz. hot
pink sugarpaste

approx. 25 g/1 oz. grass
green sugarpaste

a pink flower posy

a birdcage food stencil

a palette knife

a small paintbrush

a scribe tool

a wheel tool

a blossom plunge cutter

a ball tool

a piping bag fitted with a
very fine round nozzle/tip

1 Cover your 3 cake tiers with marzipan followed by sugarpaste, then cover your cake drum in the same sage green sugar paste (refer to pages 26 and 28–30 for full instructions).

2 Rod and stack the cake (following the instructions on page 32). Ribbon the cake drum with the gold ribbon and the cake with the pink organza ribbon, overlaid with the thinner white ribbon (see page 33).

3 Cut your birdcage stencil to size and position it firmly, but gently, just above the ribbon of the middle tier cake. Use the palette knife to smooth a thin layer of royal icing over the stencil. **(A)** Carefully remove the stencil and you will be left with a slightly raised image of the birdcage. Don't worry if the birdcages are a little rustic-looking – it tends to look prettier if the lines aren't too crisp.

4 Repeat this process, using the stencil to transfer the birdcage design all the way around the sides of the middle and base tiers. You will need to wash and dry the stencil between each birdcage image. When both tiers are completed, leave the royal icing to dry.

5 Once completely set, mix the gold lustre dust with rejuvenator fluid in a small bowl to make a paint. Use the paintbrush to carefully paint the birdcages with the gold solution **(B)**, then leave to dry.

6 Trace the lovebirds below onto separate pieces of baking parchment. Knead half the floristry paste until pliable, then roll out very thinly on an icing/confectioners' sugar-dusted surface. Hold one of the bird stencils over the floristry paste and prick along the lines with a scribe tool to mark the outline of the bird. **(C)**

7 Use a wheel tool to cut out the bird, carefully following the dotted outline. **(D)** Knead and roll out the remaining floristry paste and repeat for the other bird stencil. Leave the birds to dry for a few hours.

8 Knead and roll out the pink sugar paste on a surface dusted with icing/confectioners' sugar. Use the plunge cutter to stamp out approximately 60 blossoms. **(E)** Use the thin end of a ball tool to make an impression in the centre of each blossom – this will make the petals naturally curl up a little.

TEMPLATES

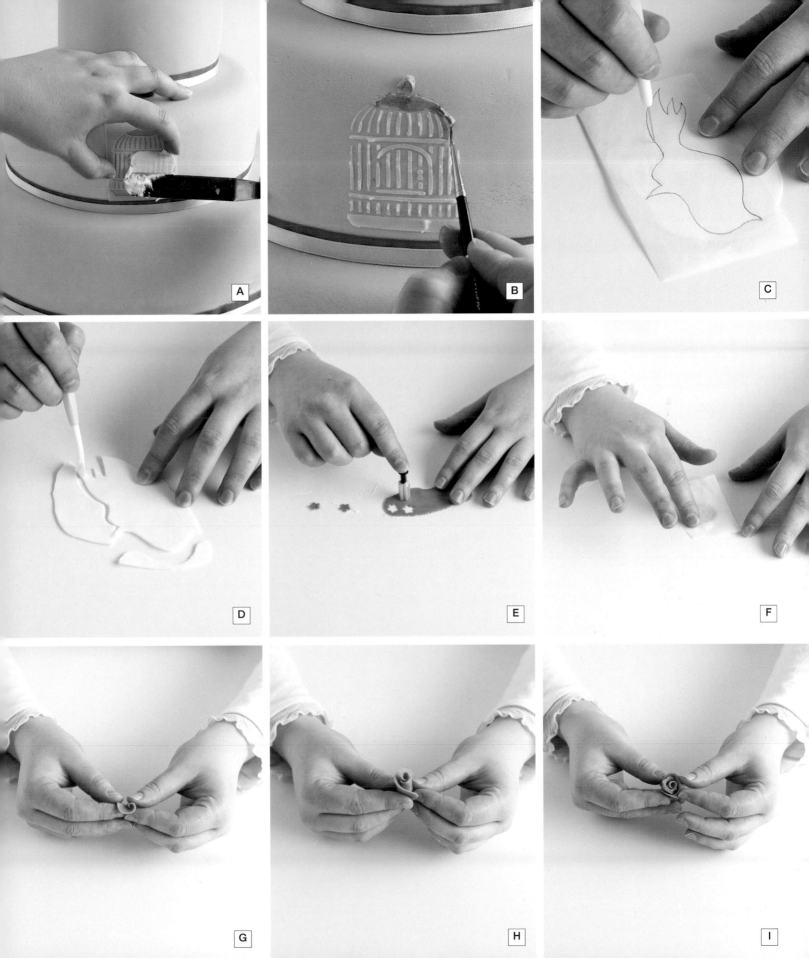

J

K

L

9 Knead more pink sugar paste to make 12 small 3-petal roses. Start by rolling a small ball (about the size of a pea) in your hands. Place it on an icing/confectioners' sugar-dusted surface, cover with a small piece of baking parchment and press out the shape of a petal. Use your finger or thumb (whichever is most comfortable) to smooth and thin out the outer edge with a circular motion, whilst keeping the petal slightly thicker at the base. **(F)** Repeat to create 2 more petals.

10 Use your thumbs and index fingers to gently roll the first petal inwards. **(G)** Gently pinch the base of the second petal and position it around the first – the sugar paste will stick to itself so there's no need for sugar glue. **(H)** Repeat with the final petal and gently use your finger and thumb to gently pinch the

edges of the petals for a more natural-looking finish. **(I)** Repeat to make 11 more roses.

11 Pinch off a small piece of of green sugar paste and shape it into a leaf. Use a clean paintbrush dampened with clear alcohol or cooled, boiled water to moisten the base of the leaf and stick it onto the base of a rose. **(J)** Repeat for the remaining roses and leave them to set.

12 Spoon more royal icing into the piping bag and pipe wings and eyes on your lovebirds. **(K)** You can create a 'fluttering eyelash' effect on the female bird by piping a pearl dot and gently dragging it upwards to create a slightly pointed tip. Leave the icing to set.

13 Use a small blob of royal icing on the back of each pink blossom to affix them to the cake, around

M

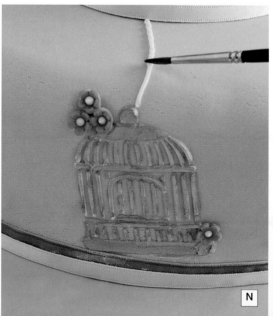

N

O

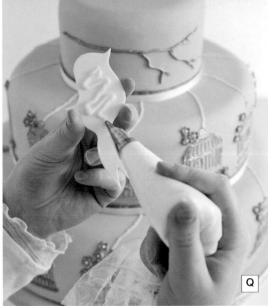

the birdcages **(L)**, reserving a few for later. Pipe a little white pearl of royal icing in the centre of each blossom.

14 Create a birdcage rope by piping a line from the ribbon edge of the tier above to connect with the top of the birdcage. **(M)** Use a paintbrush dampened with clear alcohol or cooled, boiled water to gently pat the rope to create a textured effect. **(N)** Repeat for the remaining birdcages.

15 Pipe a branch for the lovebirds to perch on in the centre of the top tier's side. For a more natural look, make the line ever so slightly wavy and pipe little offshoots from the branches. **(O)** Leave to set.

16 Mix a little more gold lustre with rejuvenator fluid and carefully paint the branch. **(P)** You can build up the colour with a few layers if necessary. Leave to dry.

17 Pipe royal icing onto the back of the lovebirds and affix them to the branch **(Q)**, positioning them so that their beaks are nearly touching.

18 Paint the piped eyes and wings of the bird with more gold paint. **(R)** (You may need to add a little more rejuvenator fluid if it has started to dry up.)

19 Finally, affix the small roses in groups of 3 on either side of the lovebirds **(S)** and on the baseboard, and add a few of the reserved pink blossoms from earlier along the occasional birdcage rope. Once ready to display, top with the posy of flowers.

Brighton Rock

This cake is inspired by the iconic confection from Britain's famous seaside town. The delicately piped stripes in pretty shades of pink, lilac and blue conjure up memories of deckchairs, the smell of the sea breeze and the sound of seagulls. The elegant white sugar roses give Brighton Rock an added elegance, befitting the occasion. I have paired this fresh, youthful design with a tasty and nostalgic peanut butter and chocolate chip cake to highlight its fun, laid-back style.

TO MAKE THE PEANUT BUTTER AND CHOCOLATE CHIP CAKE

Following the method below, prepare all 3 tiers of your cake, following the chart on page 152 to determine quantities, pan sizes and cooking times.

1 Preheat the oven to 180°C (160°C fan)/350°F (325°F fan)/Gas 4.

2 In a large mixing bowl, beat together the butter, peanut butter and sugar until pale and fluffy. Gradually add the eggs, beating well between each addition.

3 Sift the flour and baking powder over the mixture, add the salt and vanilla extract and beat together until thoroughly combined, then stir through the chocolate chips.

4 Divide the mixture evenly between the prepared cake pans and bake in the preheated oven for 20–25 minutes, or until an inserted skewer comes out clean.

5 Once baked, leave the cakes to cool in their pans on a wire rack for 10 minutes before turning out to cool completely.

6 To make the chocolate and peanut buttercream, put the butter and peanut butter in a mixing bowl and beat together with an electric whisk until pale and creamy. Sift over half the icing/confectioners' sugar and beat in, then sift over the remaining icing/confectioners' sugar and whisk again. Whisk in the cooled melted chocolate until smooth, adding a splash of milk to slacken the mixture, if required.

7 Level the cakes, if necessary (see page 25), then attach one of the cakes to the cake board with a small blob of buttercream. Sandwich the cakes together with half of the buttercream, then spread the remaining buttercream over the top and sides of the cake with a palette knife (see page 27) and leave to set.

FOR A 15-CM/6-INCH CAKE

65 g/4½ tablespoons unsalted butter, softened

35 g/2½ tablespoons smooth peanut butter

100 g/½ cup (caster) sugar

2 large eggs

100 g/¾ cup self-raising flour

1 teaspoon baking powder

a pinch of salt

1 teaspoon vanilla extract, or to taste

75 g/½ cup good quality (70% cocoa solids) dark chocolate chips

FOR THE CHOCOLATE AND PEANUT BUTTERCREAM

35 g/2½ tablespoons unsalted butter, softened

35 g/2½ tablespoons smooth peanut butter

140 g/1 cup icing/ confectioners' sugar

35 g/1¼ oz. good quality (70% cocoa solids) dark chocolate, melted and cooled

a splash of milk (optional)

2 x 15-cm/6-inch shallow round cake pans, greased and lined

a thin round cake board the same size as the cake

TO DECORATE THE CAKE

FOR THE DECORATION

marzipan (see page 157 for quantities)

white sugar paste (see page 157 for quantities), plus approx. 400 g/14 oz. extra for the posy

a cake drum 8 cm/3 inches larger than the base tier

1.5-cm/½-inch wide white satin ribbon

icing/confectioners' sugar, for dusting

2 quantities Royal Icing (see page 20)

lilac, baby blue and candy pink food colouring paste

a rose leaf punch

a cake turntable

4 piping bags fitted with small round nozzles/tips

1 Cover your 3 cake tiers with marzipan followed by sugar paste, then cover your cake drum in the same white sugar paste (refer to pages 26 and 28–30 for full instructions).

2 Rod and stack the cake (following the instructions on page 32). Ribbon the cake drum with white satin ribbon (see page 33).

3 First, make the roses – you will need about 8 to make the posy, depending on the size of the top tier. For each rose, knead a golf ball-sized piece of sugar paste until pliable. Divide it roughly into 6 pieces, making each piece slightly bigger than the last. Select the smallest piece and roll it into a small sausage shape: this will be the central petal of your rose. Roll the remaining pieces of sugar paste into balls.

4 Place the sausage shape piece of sugar paste on an icing/confectioner's sugar-dusted surface and cover with a small piece of baking paper. Pressing with your fingers or thumb (whichever you find most comfortable) flatten the sausage into an elongated

petal shape, which is thicker at the base but delicate at the tip. **(A)** Hold the base of the petal between the thumb and index finger of one hand and use the thumb and index finger of the other to gently roll the petal inwards. **(B)** It should be rolled quite tightly at the base, but loose enough at the top that the rolled edges of the petal don't stick together.

5 Select the smallest sugar paste ball and flatten it out in the same way. Gently cup the petal base between your index finger and thumb to slightly round it, then snugly wrap it around the central petal. There is no need for any sugar glue as the sugar paste will stick to itself.

6 In ascending size order, roll out all of the balls to make petals and build up the rose. As you go, use your thumb and index finger to gently pinch the edge of the petal to create natural-looking tips. **(C)**

7 Pinch off the excess sugar paste at the base of the rose. **(D)** Repeat the process until you have made 8 (or more) roses. Leave them to set overnight.

8 When you are ready to create the posy, roll out a piece of kneaded white sugar paste on a surface dusted with icing/confectioners' sugar. Use the leaf punch to stamp out 7–8 leaves. **(E)** (You will need the leaves to be pliable enough to drape, so don't make these in advance of assembling the posy.)

9 Spoon a quarter of the royal icing into one of the piping bags. To create a mound for the posy, knead a large piece of white sugar paste and roll it between your palms to shape it into a ball, then slam it down on a table to flatten the base. Pipe a generous amount of royal icing onto the base of the mound, then place it in the centre of the top tier. **(F)** Position 7 roses around the base of the mound, attaching each with a little more royal icing. **(G)**

10 Drape the leaves over the mound so that the tip of each leaf falls between 2 roses **(H)**, affixing each leaf with a blob of royal icing as you go. Finish the posy by piping a generous blob of royal icing onto the mound and placing the final rose in the centre. **(I)** If there are gaps in the top of the posy after adding the centre rose, remove the rose and add

a couple of extra petals to make the rose larger, then set in the centre again. Leave to set.

11 Divide the remaining royal icing between 3 bowls and tint them lilac, blue and pink, then fill a piping bag with each colour. Place the cake on a turntable and, starting with the top tier, pipe alternate coloured stripes down the sides of each cake. **(J, K, L)** When piping, ensure you have made contact with the cake where you wish the beginning of the line to be and then gently, but firmly, pull the nozzle slightly away from the cake, maintaining an even level of pressure, before attaching the piped line to the base of the cake. (Think of the icing like a string of spaghetti that you can just tease into the right position before making contact with the cake.) Once the stripe has been fixed, slightly increase your thumb pressure on the piping bag to create a pearl at the base on the stripe. If the line of icing has not fully attached to the cake all the way down, gently dab the line with a moist, clean paintbrush to fix it into place. Repeat this process with alternating colours until you have a fully striped three-tiered cake, then leave to set.

Jade Garden

Beautifully feminine and pretty, the summery pink and jade colour scheme leans towards chinoiserie chic. The softness of the lines, with cascading petals and full pink roses, create a graceful elegance full of delicate charm. The orange and polenta cake is deliciously moist and fresh – perfect to eat al fresco on a warm sunny day.

TO MAKE THE ORANGE POLENTA CAKE

Following the method below, prepare all 3 tiers of your cake, following the chart on page 153 to determine quantities, pan sizes and cooking times.

1 Preheat the oven to 180°C (160°C fan)/350°F (325°F fan)/Gas 4.

2 Sift together the polenta/cornmeal, flour, baking powder and salt and set aside.

3 Put the orange zest and half the orange juice in a jug/pitcher with the yogurt and sunflower oil and stir to combine.

4 In a large mixing bowl and using an electric whisk, whisk together the whole eggs, egg whites and sugar on high speed for at least 5 minutes, until thick and creamy. Beat in the orange and yogurt mixture, followed by the dry ingredients, whisking until well combined.

5 Pour the cake batter into your prepared baking pan, smooth the top level with a palette knife and bake in the preheated oven for 45–50 minutes, or until an inserted skewer comes out clean.

6 In the meantime, make the orange syrup. Put the sugar for the syrup and the remaining orange juice in a saucepan set over a gentle heat and stir until the sugar has dissolved, then increase the heat and boil for 5 minutes until the syrup has thickened slightly.

7 Once baked, place the warm cake, still in its pan, on a wire rack and stab it all over with a skewer. Pour all but 3 tablespoons of the orange syrup (keep back a little more for the larger cakes as you will need more for brushing) over the cake, then leave to cool in the pan for 30 minutes, before turning out onto the rack to cool completely.

8 When you are ready to decorate, brush the cake board with a little of the reserved orange syrup, and place the cake onto it. Brush the rest of the cake all over with the remaining orange syrup and proceed directly to the decorating instructions overleaf.

FOR A 20-CM/8-INCH CAKE

260 g/2 cups fine polenta/cornmeal

75 g/⅔ cup plain/all-purpose flour

2 teaspoons baking powder

¼ teaspoon salt

grated zest and freshly squeezed juice of 2 oranges

110 ml/scant ½ cup plain yogurt

110 ml/scant ½ cup sunflower oil

3 large eggs, plus 3 egg whites

300 g/1½ cups (caster) sugar

FOR THE ORANGE SYRUP

75 g/⅓ cup (caster) sugar

a 20-cm/8-inch deep round cake pan, greased and lined

a thin round cake board the same size as the cake

TO DECORATE THE CAKE

FOR THE DECORATION

marzipan (see page 157 for quantities)

jade sugar paste (see page 157 for quantities)

a cake drum 8 cm/3 inches larger than the base tier

1.5-cm/½-inch wide jade satin ribbon

2 teaspoons (or more if you want a stronger colour) rose pink food colouring powder

approx. ½ quantity White Modelling Chocolate (see page 23)

½ quantity Royal Icing (see page 20)

icing/confectioners' sugar, for dusting

a plastic pocket file
a disposable piping bag
a soft brush

1 Cover your 3 cake tiers with marzipan followed by sugarpaste, then cover your cake drum in the same jade sugar paste (refer to pages 26 and 28–30 for full instructions).

2 Rod and stack the cake (following the instructions on page 32), then ribbon the cake and the cake drum (see page 33).

3 Knead the colouring powder into the modelling chocolate until it is streak free, then wrap the dyed chocolate in a plastic bag and leave to rest in the fridge for 10 minutes to firm up.

4 To make a 6-petal rose, break off a golf ball-sized piece of modelling chocolate (rewrapping the remaining chocolate in the plastic bag so it doesn't dry out) and knead well until pliable. Divide it roughly into 6 pieces, each piece getting slightly bigger as you go along. Select the smallest piece and roll it into a small sausage shape: this will be the central petal of your rose. Roll the remaining pieces of chocolate into balls.

5 Cut down the edges of the plastic pocket file so that you can open it out like a book. Place all of your rolled pieces of modelling chocolate on one side of the file, with at least 5 cm/2 inches between each one, and close the file over them. Using your thumb or index and middle fingers (whichever feels most comfortable to you) press the outer edge of each piece of modelling chocolate to flatten it, to create a rose petal shape. **(A)** Try to get the outer edge as thin as possible, leaving it slightly thicker at the base of the petal. **(B)** Work quickly or the heat of your hands will cause the chocolate to stick to the plastic.

6 Once you have pressed out all of your rose petals, carefully pull back the top sheet of plastic and remove the first petal (originally the sausage-shaped piece of modelling chocolate), holding only the thicker base of the petal. Once peeled off the plastic, the petal will naturally lean backwards, so make sure you hold it with the leaning outer edges facing away from you. Hold the base of the petal between the thumb and index finger of one hand and use the thumb and index finger of the other to gently roll the petal inwards. **(C)** It should be rolled quite tightly at the base, but loose enough at the top that the rolled edges of the petal don't stick together. Using the sides of the tips of your index finger and thumb, gently soften the edges outwards to create a more natural-shaped petal.

7 Peel off the next smallest petal from your plastic file and gently cup the edges of the base of the petal between index finger and thumb to slightly round it. Snugly wrap the base of it around the first petal. There is no need for any sugar glue as the modelling chocolate will stick to itself. **(D)**

tip: personalize the cake

This cake would look beautiful in almost any colour combination, so feel free to get creative; mix and match the bride and groom's favourite colours, or choose hues which perfectly match the wedding stationery, flowers or tableware. If you would like to make the cake a little more indulgent, why not try slicing it horizontally in half and filling it with the orange blossom icing on page 91.

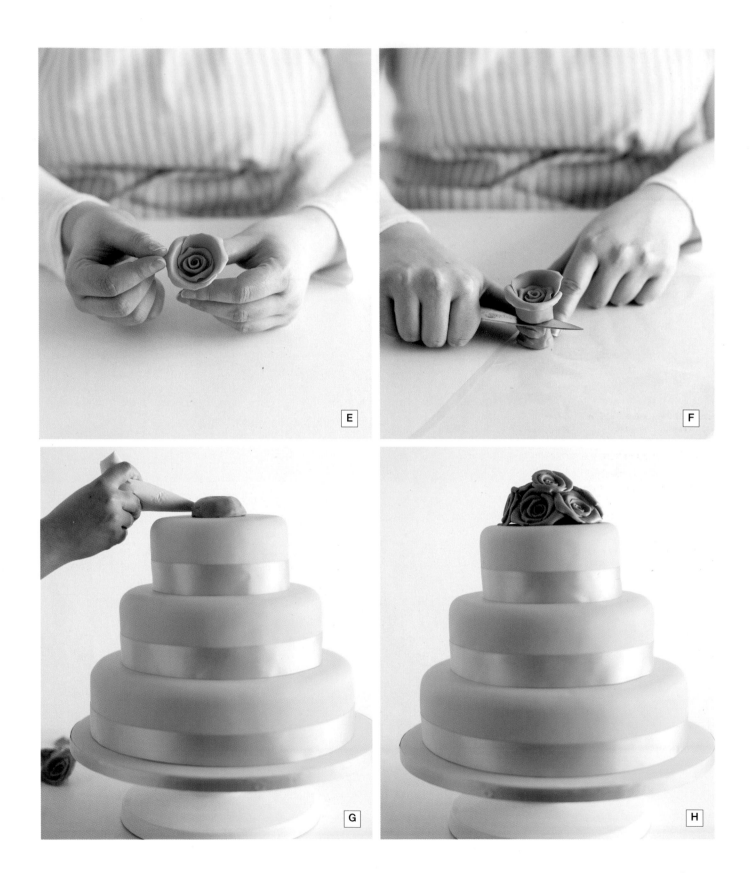

8 Repeat this process with the remaining petals, selecting the petals in ascending size order and carefully rolling each one around the rose and softening the edges between your index finger and thumb, until you are left with a full open rose. **(E)**

9 Slice off any excess modelling chocolate at the base of the rose with a small, sharp knife, being careful not to squash the petals as you go. **(F)**

10 Carry on making roses in this way, adding an extra 3 or even 6 petals to some, so you have a few very large roses. Also, leave some petals loose, so that they can tumble down the sides of the cake. When you have just a tennis ball-sized piece of chocolate remaining, stop making roses and wrap this in a plastic bag to be used later to create a mound for the top tier posy. Leave the roses and loose petals to set for about 30 minutes.

11 In the meantime, use more pink powder dye to tint the royal icing the same colour as the chocolate roses. Spoon it into the piping bag. There's no need for a nozzle as it's only going to be used as glue to stick on the roses and petals. When you're ready to use the icing, simply snip off the end of the bag.

12 Make a mound from the modelling chocolate you have set aside. The easiest way to do this is to roll it between your palms to shape it into a ball, then slam it down on a table to flatten the base. You can then tidy up its shape if necessary before affixing it to the centre of the top tier with a generous blob of royal icing. **(G)**

13 Arrange equal-sized roses in a concentric circle around the base of the mound, ensuring you have the correct number of roses to fit snugly without getting squashed. Glue each rose in place with a blob of royal icing. Finally, top the posy with another rose, so all gaps are closed and you are left with an attractive half sphere of roses. **(H)**

14 Continue to glue roses and petals evenly around the sides and edges of the rest of the tiers, securing each rose in place with royal icing. **(I)**

15 Finally, dust the finished cake with a soft brush to remove any residual icing/confectioners' sugar or ribbon fibres.

changing seasons

This chapter is a celebration of the changing beauty of the
seasons, with each design and each recipe chosen to reflect the
time of year the wedding is in. Think of the cheerful hope and
optimism of the first blue skies and birdsong of spring. Pimms
and lemonade, strawberries, reading in the park, and warm air
on sleeveless arms spell summer. Long walks, new jumpers,
kicking piles of burnt orange leaves and the smell of bonfires are
just some of autumn's charms, while winter's magic embraces
knitted scarves, the crooked smiles of snowmen and drinking
mulled wine in front of log fires.

Spring Flowers

This friendly, colourful wedding cake can't help but put a smile on your face. The bright and genial flowers climbing up the sides of the cake scream, 'Spring has sprung!' I have paired this design with a deliciously fragrant and refreshing green tea cake. The matcha gives the cake a pleasing green hue and a complex intensity of flavour, perfectly complemented by the warming heat of the ginger filling.

TO MAKE THE GREEN TEA CAKE

Following the method below, prepare all 3 tiers of your cake, following the chart on page 154 to determine quantities, pan sizes and cooking times.

1 Preheat the oven to 180°C (160°C fan)/350°F (325°F fan)/Gas 4.

2 Put all the cake ingredients in a large mixing bowl and whisk for a couple of minutes with an electric whisk, until everything is well combined, light and fluffy. You can add a splash of milk to slightly slacken the mixture at this stage, if required, but be careful not to overbeat the mixture or your cake will have a dense, bready texture.

3 Divide the batter between the prepared cake pans and bake in the centre of the preheated oven for 20–25 minutes, or until an inserted skewer comes out clean.

4 Leave the cakes to cool in their pans, set on a wire rack, for 10 minutes before turning out onto the rack to cool completely.

5 To make the ginger buttercream, whisk the butter with an electric whisk until fluffy. Sift over half the icing/confectioners' sugar and whisk again until fully incorporated. Whisk through the ginger syrup before sifting over the remaining icing/confectioners' sugar and whisking through. Add the cream cheese and whisk again until light and fluffy. You can add a little more ginger syrup to slightly slacken the mixture at this stage, if necessary, but you need the filling to be spreadable, not runny. Finally, fold through the chopped stem ginger.

6 Level the cakes, if necessary (see page 25), then attach one of the cakes to the cake board with a small blob of the buttercream. Sandwich the cakes together with half of the buttercream, then spread the remaining buttercream over the top and sides of the cake with a palette knife (see page 27) and leave to set.

FOR A 15-CM/6-INCH CAKE

100 g/6½ tablespoons unsalted butter, softened

100 g/½ cup (caster) sugar

2 large eggs

75 g/⅔ cup self-raising flour, sifted

1 teaspoon baking powder

25 g/¼ cup ground almonds

1 tablespoon matcha powder

a splash of milk (optional)

FOR THE GINGER BUTTERCREAM

35 g/2½ tablespoons unsalted butter, softened

100 g/¾ cup icing/confectioners' sugar

1–2 tablespoons ginger syrup*

15 g/1 tablespoon Philadelphia cream cheese (see page 4)

1 ball of Chinese stem ginger, finely chopped

2 x 15-cm/6-inch shallow round cake pans, greased and lined

a thin round cake board the same size as the cake

* This can be drained from the stem ginger jar or you can make your own following the instructions on page 145.

TO DECORATE THE CAKE

FOR THE DECORATION

marzipan (see page 157 for quantities)

white sugar paste (see page 157 for quantities), plus a little extra for the bluebells

a cake drum 8 cm/3 inches larger than the base tier

1.5-cm/½-inch wide white satin ribbon

approx. 150 g/5 oz. white floristry paste

daffodil yellow, bluebell*, and red food colouring pastes

cornflour/cornstarch, for dusting

clear alcohol (such as vodka)

tangerine-coloured edible lustre dust

rejuvenator fluid

½ quantity Royal Icing (see page 20)

approx. 125 g/4½ oz. grass green sugar paste

large and small daffodil cutters

a ball tool

a wheel tool

a shallow paint palette (optional)

a paintbrush

a piping bag fitted with a small round nozzle/tip

a small star cutter

cocktail sticks/toothpicks

large and small rose petal cutters

a foam modelling mat

a scribe tool

* If you can't find bluebell food colouring paste, you can create it by mixing blue and violet dyes.

1 Cover your 3 cake tiers with marzipan followed by sugar paste, then cover your cake drum in the same white sugar paste (refer to pages 26 and 28–30 for full instructions).

2 Rod and stack the cake (following the instructions on page 32), then ribbon the cake and the cake drum (see page 33).

3 Tint approximately half of the floristry paste daffodil yellow. (Store the remaining floristry paste in a plastic bag so it doesn't dry out.) On a surface dusted with cornflour/cornstarch, roll out the yellow floristry paste very thinly.

4 Using the large daffodil cutters, stamp out 2 sets of petals and 1 central bell for each daffodil – you will need 3 large daffodils.

5 Repeat step 4 using the small daffodil cutter, stamping out enough petals and bells to make 3 small daffodils. **(A)** (Reserve any remaining yellow floristry paste for the tulip centres, storing it in a plastic bag to keep it from drying out).

6 Using a ball tool, roll each petal from the centre point outwards **(B)**, then score a faint line along the centre of each petal using the wheel tool. Leave the petals to dry in a shallow paint palette (or similar) – you want the edges of the petals to be just slightly raised, you don't want to create a deep dip.

7 For the central bell, roll the ball tool firmly over the outer edges of the petal, holding the base with your fingers and rolling away from you to create a crinkled effect. Wet the edge of one end of the piece with a paintbrush dampened with clear alcohol and curl it round, pressing the edges together to form the characteristic trumpet. **(C)** Repeat for all the bells.

8 Mix a little tangerine lustre dust with rejuvenator fluid in a small bowl and use a paintbrush to gently brush it onto to the central bells of the small daffodils. **(D)** Leave all the bells to set.

9 Spoon the royal icing into a piping bag. Assemble the large daffodils by stacking 2 of the large petal pieces to create a 6-petalled flower. Stick the petals together with a blob of icing from the piping bag, then attach a large central bell with another dab of icing. **(E)** Repeat this process to create 2 more large and 3 small daffodils.

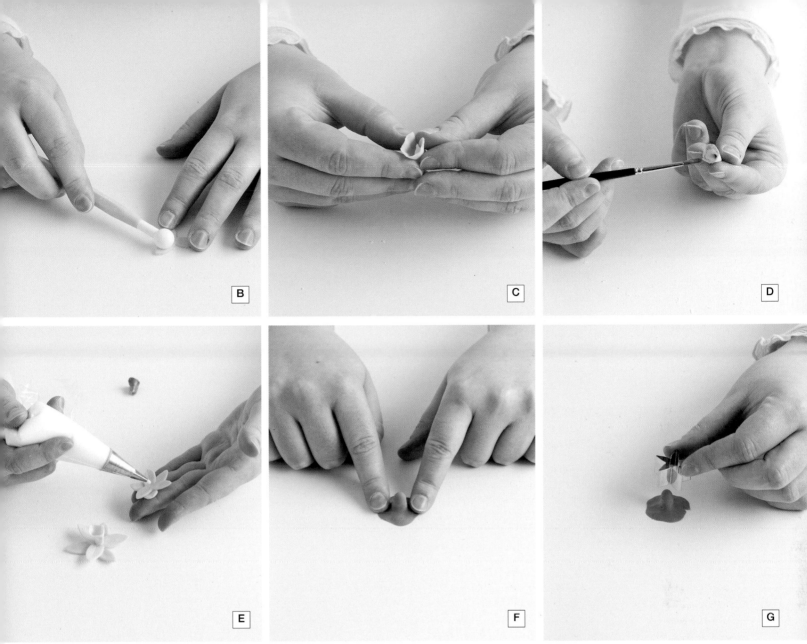

10 To make the bluebells, knead together a third of the remaining white floristry paste with the same quantity of white sugar paste and enough bluebell food dye to create a vivid colour. Take a small piece of the bluebell paste (sealing the remainder in a plastic bag) and mould it into a Mexican hat shape. **(F)** Place the star cutter over the hat to cut a star shape into the brim **(G)**, removing the trimmings.

11 Roll the tip of each star up around a cocktail stick/toothpick to create a curled petal. **(H)** Repeat, making enough bluebells to fill 3 large stems, then leave them to set.

I

J

K

12 To make the tulips, begin by creating a teardrop shape with yellow floristry paste. Taper the narrow end of the teardrop into a long, pointy tip. **(I)**

13 To make the petals, tint the remaining white floristry paste red and roll it out thinly on a cornflour/cornstarch-dusted surface. Using the rose petal cutters, cut 3 of each size petal for each tulip. **(J)** You will need 3 tulips (therefore 18 petals) in total.

14 In turn, place each petal on the foam modelling mat and roll over it with a ball tool to give it a more natural shape. **(K)** Press the side of a scribe tool onto each petal to create vertical indentations running lengthways from the tip. Leave the small petals to dry over teaspoons and the large petals to dry over dessertspoons. **(L)**

15 Spoon the royal icing into a piping bag. Attach the 3 small petals around the base of the yellow tulip centre, gluing each with a blob of royal icing. **(M)** When the icing has set a little, attach the larger petals around the flower **(N)** and leave it to set

L

M

N

completely. Repeat until you have assembled all 3 tulips, then leave the flowers to set.

16 To make the flower stems, knead small pieces of green sugar paste until pliable, then use your fingers to roll them out into long, thin sausages of an even width all the way along. In this way, create stems of varying heights and widths for each daffodil, tulip and bluebell. Curve each bluebell stem into a lower case 'r' shape.

17 For the leaves, knead and roll out more green sugar paste into sausages which taper to a point at the ends. Flatten the sausage and trim one end on the diagonal so it will sit against the flower stem or the base of the cake at an angle. Roll a wheel tool gently along the leaf to create veins.

18 Attach the stems and leaves to the cake with a paintbrush dipped in clear alcohol. The tulip stems should protrude above edges of the tiers so that the flower heads can be positioned on the lip of the tier above. **(O)**

19 Attach the daffodils **(P)** and tulips **(Q)** to the top of their stems with a blob of royal icing. Affix generous clusters of bluebells to the curved stems, so they appear to be weighing down the stem **(R)**, then leave the cake to set completely.

Summer Fete

This irresistibly cheerful cake conjures up the innocent fun of a village celebration: mismatched chairs and china; pretty dresses; dancing to a slightly out-of-tune piano. It's perfect for a summer wedding in the country, and the bunting can be painted to match the wedding colours, or, to really set it off, why not fill the entire venue with bunting that matches the cake? I've paired this with a classic English tearoom confection: the lemon drizzle. This light and zesty cake is one of Victoria's Cake Boutique's most popular requests, and is a sure-fire winner with everyone, young and old.

TO MAKE THE LEMON DRIZZLE CAKE

Following the method below, prepare all 3 tiers of your cake, following the chart on page 153 to determine quantities, pan sizes and cooking times.

1 Preheat the oven to 180°C (160°C fan)/350°F (325°F fan)/Gas 4.

2 In a large mixing bowl and using an electric whisk, beat together all the cake ingredients except the lemon zest and curd, until pale and fluffy, then fold through the lemon zest.

3 Pour the batter into the prepared cake pan and bake in the preheated oven for 30–35 minutes, or until an inserted skewer comes out clean.

4 While the cake is baking, make the lemon 'drizzle'. In a jug/pitcher, stir together the lemon juice and sugar, then leave to stand.

5 Once baked, place the warm cake, still in its pan, on a wire rack and stab it all over with a skewer. Give the lemon drizzle a quick stir, before pouring it over the top of the hot cake. (For larger cakes, drizzle over the syrup in 2 stages, allowing the first half to soak in before drizzling over the remaining syrup. This will prevent syrup-sodden sides and a dry middle.) Leave the cake to cool completely in its pan before turning out and levelling, if necessary (see page 25).

6 When you are ready to decorate the cake, brush a little of the warmed lemon curd onto the cake board and set the cake onto it. Brush lemon curd all over the rest of the cake, then proceed directly to the decorating instructions overleaf.

FOR A 15-CM/6-INCH CAKE

100 g/6½ tablespoons unsalted butter, softened

150 g/¾ cup (caster) sugar

150g/1¼ cups self-raising flour

1 teaspoon baking powder

2 large eggs

60 ml/¼ cup whole milk

finely grated zest of 2 lemons

45 g/3 tablespoons lemon curd, warmed

FOR THE LEMON DRIZZLE

freshly squeezed juice of 2 lemons

100 g/½ cup (caster) sugar

a 15-cm/6-inch deep round cake pan, greased and lined

a thin round cake board the same size as the cake

FOR THE DECORATION

marzipan (see page 157 for quantities)

white sugar paste (see page 157 for quantities)

a cake drum 8 cm/3 inches larger than the base tier

1.5-cm/½-inch wide white satin ribbon

a black edible ink pen

approx. 100 g/3½ oz. white floristry paste

cornflour/cornstarch, for dusting

approx. 50 g/3 tablespoons cocoa butter powder

edible lustre dusts

½ quantity Royal Icing (see page 20)

a scribe tool

a wheel tool

a paint palette or plate

a few clean paintbrushes

a piping bag fitted with a small round nozzle/tip

TO DECORATE THE CAKE

1 Cover your 3 cake tiers with marzipan followed by sugar paste, then cover your cake drum in the same white sugar paste (refer to pages 26 and 28–30 for full instructions).

2 Rod and stack the cake (following the instructions on page 32), then ribbon the cake and the cake drum (see page 33).

3 Using a scribe tool, carefully mark out evenly spaced swags around all 3 tiers of the cake. When you are satisfied they are even, draw swags directly onto the cake using the edible ink pen. **(A)** Draw a little bow at the meeting point of each swag.

4 Knead the floristry paste, then roll it out on a cornflour/cornstarch-dusted surface, until very thin. Use a wheel tool to cut the paste into 2.5-cm/1-inch wide strips, then use diagonal cuts to form triangles for the bunting flags. **(B)** Measure how many flags fill each swag and multiply that by the number of swags, and include a few spares for your patch kit (see page 14). Leave them to dry overnight.

5 Melt the cocoa butter powder in a heatproof bowl set over a saucepan of barely simmering water. Tip a little of each coloured dust into the palette and mix in a little melted cocoa butter to make a selection of coloured paints. Paint the bunting flags with a solid colour or personalize them with your own designs. **(C)** Once painted, leave the flags to dry.

6 Spoon the royal icing into the piping bag and pipe a swirl onto the back of each flag **(D)**, pressing them gently into place on the cake as you go. **(E)**

Autumn Hedgerow

FOR AN 18-CM/7-INCH CAKE

5 large eggs, separated

120 g/²⁄₃ cup (caster) sugar

180 g/1¾ cups ground almonds

180 g/6¼ oz. white chocolate, melted

120 ml/½ cup raspberry purée*

120 ml/½ cup blackcurrant purée*

60 ml/¼ cup blackberry purée*

¼ teaspoon salt

FOR THE BERRY GANACHE

120 g/4¼ oz. good quality (70% cocoa solids) dark chocolate, chopped

120 g/1 stick unsalted butter

120 ml/½ cup berry purée (a mixture of raspberry, blackberry and blackcurrant)

120 ml/½ cup double/ heavy cream

40 g/3 tablespoons light muscovado sugar

2 x 18-cm/7-inch shallow round cake pans, greased and lined

a thin round cake board the same size as the cake

* You can buy ready-made fruit purées, but if you prefer, make your own following the recipe in the tip box opposite.

Autumn's harvest is bountiful with soft hedgerow berries of bramble, elder and hawthorn, ready to be picked by gloved fingers and made into jam. Inspired by nature, these hand-moulded and hand-painted white chocolate blackberries are stunningly naturalistic. This cake will have your guests queuing to get a closer look, so they can marvel at your creative handiwork. I have paired this design with a delectably tangy fruits of the forest torte, filled with fruity berry and chocolate ganache: a sumptuous and sophisticated autumnal dessert.

TO MAKE THE FRUITS OF THE FOREST TORTE

Following the method below, prepare all 3 tiers of your cake, following the chart on page 155 to determine quantities, pan sizes and cooking times.

1 Preheat the oven to 170°C (150°C fan)/325°F (300°F fan)/Gas 3.

2 In a large mixing bowl and using an electric whisk, beat together the egg yolks and sugar until pale and mousse-like. Whisk through the ground almonds, followed by the chocolate and fruit purées.

3 In a separate spotlessly clean bowl, whisk the egg whites with the salt until they form stiff peaks. Fold the egg whites into the cake batter until well combined, being careful not to beat the air out of the mixture.

4 Pour the batter into your prepared cake pans and bake in the preheated oven for 35–40 minutes, or until an inserted skewer comes out clean.

5 Leave the cakes to cool in their pans, set on a wire rack, for 10 minutes before turning out onto the rack to cool completely.

6 To make the ganache, melt the chocolate and butter together in a heatproof bowl set over a pan of barely simmering water. Remove from the heat and stir in the fruit purée.

7 Put the cream and sugar in a saucepan set over a gentle heat and stir until the sugar has dissolved, then bring the cream to the boil. Pour the hot cream over the chocolate mixture and stir until combined. Leave the ganache to cool, then, once cold, refrigerate until it has set.

8 Level the cakes, if necessary (see page 25), then attach one of the cakes to the cake board with a small blob of berry ganache. Sandwich the cakes together with half of the ganache, then spread the remaining ganache over the top and sides of the cake with a palette knife (see page 27) and leave to set.

tip: making berry purée

To make the berry purée, put 500 g/1 lb. 2 oz. blackcurrants, blackberries or raspberries in a food processor with 50 g/¼ cup sugar (or 100 g/½ cup sugar if using blackcurrants, as they are sharper) and pulse until the fruit has completely broken down. Pass the purée through a fine sieve/strainer to remove the seeds, then use as per the recipe above. *Makes approximately 350 ml/1⅓ cups.*

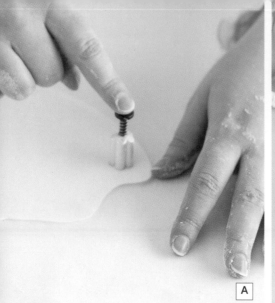

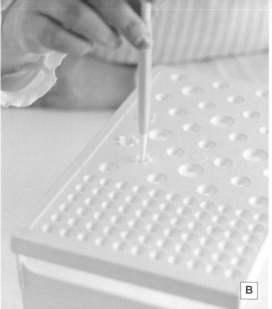

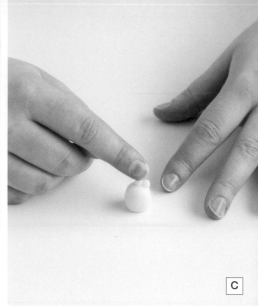

A

B

C

FOR THE DECORATION

marzipan (see page 157 for quantities)

white sugar paste (see page 157 for quantities)

a cake drum 8 cm/3 inches larger than the base tier

1.5-cm/½-inch wide white satin ribbon

approx. 30 g/1 oz. white floristry paste

cornflour/cornstarch, for dusting

1 quantity White Modelling Chocolate (see page 23)

clear alcohol, such as vodka (optional)

½ quantity Royal Icing (see page 20)

approx. 50 g/3 tablespoons cocoa butter powder

edible lustre dusts in red, green, brown, blackberry, yellow, purple and pink

a blossom plunge cutter

a folding flower stand

a ball tool

a paintbrush

cocktail sticks/toothpicks

a silicone blackberry leaf mould

a small calyx cutter

a piping bag fitted with a small round nozzle/tip

a paint palette or plate

TO DECORATE THE CAKE

1 Cover your 3 cake tiers with marzipan followed by sugar paste, then cover your cake drum in the same white sugar paste (refer to pages 26 and 28–30 for full instructions).

2 Rod and stack the cake (following the instructions on page 32), then ribbon the cake and the cake drum (see page 33).

3 To make the blackberry flowers, knead the floristry paste until pliable and roll it out very thinly on a cornflour/cornstarch-dusted surface. Stamp out 10–15 blossoms (depending on the size of your cake). **(A)** Press each blossom gently into a small hole in the folding flower stand with the small end of a ball tool **(B)**, and leave them to dry overnight.

4 To make the blackberries, start with a small dome-shaped mound of white modelling chocolate. Roll tiny balls of modelling chocolate and use them to cover the dome. **(C)** (The chocolate should stick to itself, but if it needs a little help, use a paintbrush dipped in a little alcohol to dampen the dome first.) Once the top half of the blackberry is covered, skewer it onto a cocktail stick/toothpick and it will be much easier to continue adding balls to the underside of the berry. **(D)** When the blackberry is completely covered, secure the cocktail stick/toothpick in a spare lump of sugar paste **(E)** (or you could use a potato, or similar). Make 15–25 blackberries and leave them to dry.

5 To make the blackberry leaves, dust the silicone leaf mould lightly with cornflour/cornstarch, then

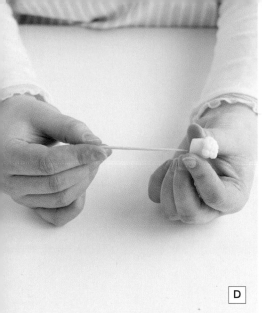

D

E

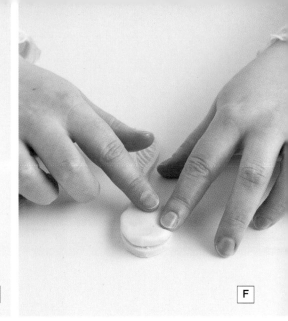

F

press a small piece of modelling chocolate into the mould. **(F)** Close the mould and press the sides together firmly so any excess chocolate is squeezed out, then tear the excess away to leave a rough edge on the leaf. **(G)** Turn the leaf out of the mould. **(H)**

6 Make calyxes for the blackberry flowers by rolling out a piece of modelling chocolate on a cornflour/cornstarch-dusted surface and stamping out calyxs with the cutter. Shape each calyx with a ball tool **(I)** and leave to dry. Make as many calyxs as you have blackberry flowers.

7 For the bramble vine, roll a large ball of modelling chocolate into a long, slim sausage shape. You can create the vine in 1 piece or roll smaller lengths and build it up on the cake, if that is easier. Wrap the vine around the cake and secure it with royal icing. **(J)**

8 Next, create the thorns for the vine by pinching small pieces of modelling chocolate into triangles, and position the thorns along the vine. **(K)** (Again, the chocolate should be self-sticking, but dampen the vine with a little clear alcohol if it needs a little help – this often depends on the temperature of the room you are working in.) Once all thorns have been positioned, gently scratch the vine all over with a scribe tool to create a natural-looking texture.

9 Melt the cocoa butter powder in a heatproof bowl set over a saucepan of barely simmering water. Mix the melted cocoa with the lustre dusts to create a palette of various hues of green, yellow, brown and red. Paint the vine with the edible paint, creating a natural look by building up the different hues rather than using a solid colour, then leave to dry. **(L)**

G

H

I

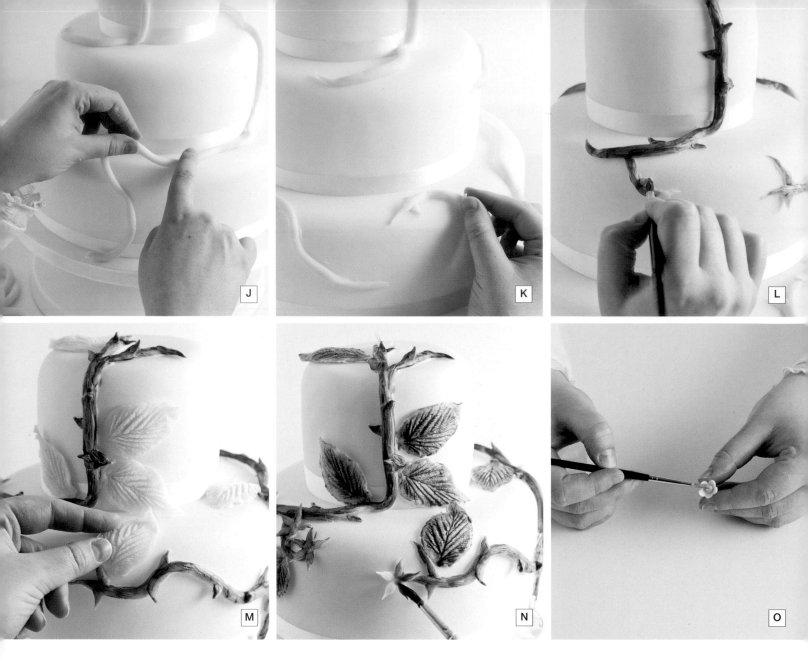

10 Attach the leaves and calyxs to the vine with blobs of royal icing and leave to set **(M)**, then paint them as you have the rest of the vine. **(N)** (If the paint dries up at any point, it can be revived by gently reheating it to melt the cocoa butter.)

11 Pipe a small blob of royal icing into the centre of each blossom and leave to dry.

12 While the cake and blossoms are drying, melt some more cocoa butter to paint the blackberry flowers and berries. Paint the centre of the flowers yellow, then, when dry, paint tiny spots of brown in the yellow centre for the stamens. **(O)** Leave to dry.

13 Use a palette of blackberry, purple, red and pink (plus a little green for under-ripe berries) edible dusts mixed with melted cocoa butter to paint the blackberries, then leave to dry. **(P)**

14 Use a blob of royal icing from the piping bag to attach a blackberry flower onto each calyx. **(Q)**

15 If you would like to add a little more detail, you can paint delicate extensions of the vines directly onto the cake with a paintbrush. **(R)**

16 Finally, attach the blackberries around the vines with a little more royal icing **(S)**, then leave the cake to set completely.

Winter Wonderland

This spectacular pale blue cake shimmers with iridescent lustre and cascading pearly snowflakes. This glimmering, icy cake evokes memories of crunching through freshly laid snow in wellington boots, the smell of pine trees at Christmas, dark nights and the glow of candlelight. I have paired this elegant design with a chestnut cake, sweetened with honey and filled with deliciously rich and nutty chestnut cream cheese icing. Scrumptiously seasonal for a sparkling Winter wedding.

FOR A 23-CM/9-INCH CAKE

100 g/½ cup (caster) sugar

100 g/6½ tablespoons runny honey

8 large eggs, separated

75 g/5 tablespoons unsalted butter, melted and cooled slightly

100 g/⅔ cup blanched hazelnuts, roasted and ground

100 g/¾ cup plus 2 tablespoons chestnut flour

¼ teaspoon salt

FOR THE CHESTNUT FROSTING

75 g/5 tablespoons unsalted butter, softened

75 g/5 tablespoons Philadelphia cream cheese (see page 4)

500 g/1 lb. 2 oz. sweet chestnut purée*

400 g/3 cups icing/ confectioners' sugar

2 x 23-cm/9-inch shallow round cake pans, greased and lined

a thin round cake board the same size as the cake

* You can buy ready-made chestnut purée, but if you prefer, make your own following the recipe in the tip box opposite.

TO MAKE THE CHESTNUT CAKE

Following the method below, prepare all 3 tiers of your cake, following the chart on page 156 to determine quantities, pan sizes and cooking times.

1 Preheat the oven to 160°C (145°C fan)/325°F (300°F fan)/Gas 3.

2 In a large mixing bowl and using an electric whisk, beat together the sugar, honey and egg yolks to the ribbon stage – pale, thick and mousse-like and the mixture leaves a slowly disappearing trail when you lift the beaters (this will take a good few minutes, so be patient). Then whisk in the melted butter, before folding in the ground hazelnuts and chestnut flour.

3 In a separate spotlessly-clean bowl, whisk the egg whites with the salt until they form stiff peaks. Using a large metal spoon, fold the egg whites into the batter, being careful not to knock the air out of the mixture.

4 Divide the batter between the prepared cake pans and bake in the preheated oven for 45–50 minutes, or until an inserted skewer comes out clean.

5 Once baked, leave the cakes to cool in their pans, set on a wire rack, for 10 minutes before turning out onto the rack to cool completely.

6 To make the filling, whisk together the butter, cream cheese and half of the chestnut purée. Sift over half the icing/confectioners' sugar and whisk until combined, then sift over the remaining icing/ confectioners' sugar and whisk again until smooth and creamy. Fold in the remaining chestnut purée lightly, leaving ripples of the purée still visible running through the frosting.

7 Level the cakes, if necessary (see page 25), then attach one of the cakes to the cake board with a small blob of frosting. Sandwich the cakes together with half of the frosting, then spread the remaining frosting over the top and sides of the cake with a palette knife (see page 27) and leave to set.

tip: making chestnut purée

Place 250 g/9 oz. peeled chestnuts, 175 ml/⅔ cup plus 1 tablespoon whole milk and 1 vanilla pod and seeds in a saucepan and bring to the boil. Reduce the heat and leave to simmer for about 30 minutes, or until soft. Remove the vanilla pod, add the 50 g/¼ cup (caster) sugar and blend to a smooth purée in a food processor. Leave to cool. *Makes 500 g/1 lb. 2 oz.*

TO DECORATE THE CAKE

FOR THE DECORATION

marzipan (see page 157 for quantities)

chestnut liqueur or dark rum (optional)

pale blue sugar paste (see page 157 for quantities)

a cake drum 8 cm/3 inches larger than the base tier

approx. 150 g/5½ oz. white floristry paste

cornflour/cornstarch, for dusting

snowflake edible lustre dust

rejuvenator fluid

1.5-cm/½-inch wide white satin ribbon

1 quantity Royal Icing (see page 20)

3 snowflake punch stamps in different sizes

a small paintbrush

a piping bag fitted with a small round nozzle/tip

1 Cover your 3 cake tiers with marzipan (you can brush the cake with chestnut liqueur or dark rum to stick on the marzipan if the buttercream is too set), followed by sugar paste, then cover your cake drum in the same blue sugar paste (see pages 26 and 28–30 for full instructions).

2 Knead a piece of floristry paste until pliable, then roll out very thinly on a surface dusted with cornflour/cornstarch. Using the snowflake punch stamps, cut out between 20 and 30 snowflakes, or more for a larger or more fully snowflake-covered cake. **(A)** Leave the snowflakes to dry overnight.

3 In a small bowl, mix the snowflake lustre dust with a little rejuvenator fluid and use a paintbrush to paint the snowflakes with the solution. **(B)** Leave to dry. For a stronger shimmer, you can build up extra layers of lustre, allowing each snowflake to dry before painting on the next layer.

4 Rub your cakes and the iced cake drum with the lustre dust to create a shimmering surface **(C)**, then rub the satin ribbon with the lustre dust.

5 Rod and stack the cake (following the instructions on page 32), then ribbon the cake and the cake drum with the shimmering ribbon (see page 33). **(D)**

6 Spoon the royal icing into the piping bag and attach the snowflakes to the cake with a dab of royal icing on their backs, creating a cascading effect down one side. **(E)** Leave to set completely.

E

quantity charts

You can find the different recipe methods for each cake within the main project pages, but I have provided quantity charts here with the ingredients for a large selection of alternative sized cake pans. Once you have decided which cakes you want to make, and followed the portion guide below to work out how big they need to be, you can head to the quantity charts, which have all been kept together in one handy section for easy reference.

The number of guests will be the guiding factor in how big the cake will need to be, along with whether the cake is to be served as dessert or with coffee later in the evening. Don't forget to take into consideration whether the bride and groom are planning to save their top tier, as you will need to subtract this from the portioning.

Make sure your tier sizes increase with even graduation, so that you are left with the same sized 'lip' on each tier (for example, a cake with 15-cm/6-inch, 20-cm/8-inch and 25-cm/10-inch tiers will mean an even 2.5-cm/1-inch lip all the way around on each tier.) To do this, you may need to make slightly more cake than needed, but a little bit of extra cake is always preferable to not enough. Some people opt for a larger than needed cake to create a stronger sense of drama with the design and they don't usually have any difficulties finding a grateful home for any leftovers. For very large weddings, you can opt to make extra cutting cakes to ensure there is enough cake to feed everyone. These cakes are iced but not decorated and are kept in the kitchen ready to be cut and served by the caterers.

	Coffee portions		Dessert portions	
Cake size	Round	Square	Round	Square
10 cm/4 inch	10	15	3	4
13 cm/5 inch	15	20	5	7
15 cm/6 inch	25	25	10	15
18 cm/7 inch	30	40	15	20
20 cm/8 inch	40	50	20	30
23 cm/9 inch	50	65	30	40
25 cm/10 inch	60	80	35	50
28 cm/11 inch	70	95	45	60
30 cm/12 inch	80	100	50	70
33 cm/13 inch	90	110	55	75
35 cm/14 inch	100	125	60	80

A Note On Measurements:

All teaspoon and tablespoon measurements are level, unless otherwise specified. Please don't be tempted to use any old spoons you find rattling around in your cutlery drawer, or your results may be affected. If you do not already own a set, it's worth investing in accurate kitchen measuring spoons. Although raising agents should be measured in accordance with the recipe instructions, there is a little more leeway for flavourings. The measurements of vanilla extract, citrus zest, coffee or spices are largely down to personal taste, so feel free to adjust my recipes accordingly. It's a good idea to get into the habit of tasting your batters and fillings for flavour, before baking or covering cakes.

Occasionally I use the term 'splash' for the addition of milk to loosen a batter. This is a deliberately vague measurement as the amount of milk needed is variable. This can depend on the size of the eggs you use, which, although categorized by size, are natural, unique products that cannot be regimentally measured, or the firmness of your butter, which can be season or weather dependent. As a rough guide, a 'splash' is around 1–2 tablespoons, but judging by eye will give far more accurate results. Learn to trust your own common sense and all will be well.

broadway melody

For the Victorian Fruitcake (to be prepared in 1 deep cake pan)

INGREDIENTS	13 cm/5 inch square (15 cm/6 inch round)	18 cm/7 inch square (20 cm/8 inch round)	20 cm/8 inch square (23 cm/9 inch round)	23 cm/9 inch square (25 cm/10 inch round)	28 cm/11 inch square (30 cm/12 inch round)
currants	75 g/½ cup	110 g/¾ cup	150 g/1 cup	225 g/1½ cups	300 g/2 cups
sultanas/golden raisins	100 g/⅔ cup	150 g/1 cup	200 g/1⅓ cups	300 g/2 cups	400 g/2⅔ cups
seedless raisins	150 g/1 cup	225 g/1½ cups	300 g/2 cups	450 g/3 cups	600 g/4 cups
dried sour cherries or cranberries	25 g/2½ tablespoons	40 g/¼ cup	50 g/⅓ cup	75 g/½ cup	100 g/⅔ cup
Medjool dates	75 g/2½ oz.	115 g/4 oz.	150 g/5½ oz.	225 g/8 oz.	300 g/10½ oz.
glacé/candied cherries	50 g/⅓ cup	75 g/½ cup	100 g/⅔ cup	150 g/1 cup	200 g/1⅓ cups
balls of stem ginger	3	4½	6	9	12
brandy or dark rum	75 ml/5 tablespoons	115 ml/scant ½ cup	150 ml/⅔ cup	225 ml/scant 1 cup	300 ml/1¼ cups
espresso	1 tablespoon	1½ tablespoons	2 tablespoons	3 tablespoons	4 tablespoons
vanilla extract	1 teaspoon	2 teaspoons	1 tablespoon	1½ tablespoons	2 tablespoons
large oranges	1	1½	2	3	4
unsalted butter	75 g/5 tablespoons	100 g/6½ tablespoons	150 g/1 stick plus 2 tablespoons	225 g/2 sticks	300 g/2½ sticks
molasses sugar	50 g/¼ cup packed	75 g/⅓ cup packed	100 g/½ cup packed	150 g/¾ cup packed	200 g/1 cup packed
large eggs	1	1	2	3	4
plain/all-purpose flour	125 g/1 cup	185 g/1½ cups	250 g/2 cups	375 g/3 cups	500 g/4 cups
ground cinnamon	1 teaspoon	1½ teaspoons	2 teaspoons	1 tablespoon	1½ tablespoons
ground ginger	1 teaspoon	1½ teaspoons	2 teaspoons	1 tablespoon	1½ tablespoons
mixed/apple-pie spice	2 teaspoons	1 tablespoon	1½ tablespoons	2 tablespoons	3 tablespoons
grated nutmeg	½ teaspoon	¾ teaspoon	1 teaspoon	1½ teaspoons	2 teaspoons
ground almonds	50 g/½ cup	75 g/¾ cup	100 g/1 cup	150 g/1½ cups	200 g/2 cups
salt	a pinch	¼ teaspoon	½ teaspoon	¾ teaspoon	1 teaspoon
bicarbonate of soda/ baking soda	a pinch	½ teaspoon	¾ teaspoon	1 teaspoon	1½ teaspoons
water	1 teaspoon	½ tablespoon	1 tablespoon	1½ tablespoons	2 tablespoons
extra brandy or dark rum for steeping*	1 tablespoon	1½ tablespoons	2 tablespoons	3 tablespoons	4 tablespoons
apricot jam	100 g/⅓ cup	140 g/½ cup	190 g/⅔ cup	250 g/scant 1 cup	400 g/1⅓ cups
baking time	1 hour at 160°C (145°C fan)/325°F (300°F fan)/ Gas 3, then cover and reduce the oven to 150°C (135°C fan)/ 300°F (275°F fan) Gas 2 and bake for a further 1¼ hours.	1 hour at 160°C (145°C fan)/325°F (300°F fan)/ Gas 3, then cover and reduce the oven to 150°C (135°C fan)/ 300°F (275°F fan) Gas 2 and bake for a further 2 hours.	1 hour at 160°C (145°C fan)/325°F (300°F fan)/ Gas 3, then cover and reduce the oven to 150°C (135°C fan)/ 300°F (275°F fan) Gas 2 and bake for a further 2½ hours.	1 hour at 160°C (145°C fan)/325°F (300°F fan)/ Gas 3, then cover and reduce the oven to 150°C (135°C fan)/ 300°F (275°F fan) Gas 2 and bake for a further 3¼ hours.	1 hour at 160°C (145°C fan)/325°F (300°F fan)/ Gas 3, then cover and reduce the oven to 150°C (135°C fan)/ 300°F (275°F fan) Gas 2 and bake for a further 4½ hours.

* If you are maturing the cake, drizzle over the same quantity again each week, as per the instructions on page 40.

For the Chocolate Fudge Cake (to be prepared in 2 shallow cake pans)

INGREDIENTS	15 cm/6 inch round (13 cm/5 inch square)	20 cm/8 inch round (18 cm/7 inch square)	25 cm/10 inch round (23 cm/9 inch square)	30 cm/12 inch round (28 cm/11 inch square)	35 cm/14 inch round (33 cm/13 inch square)
whole milk	100 ml/⅓ cup	200 ml/¾ cup	400 ml/1⅔ cups	600 ml/2½ cups	800 ml/3⅓ cups
dark chocolate	50 g/1¾ oz.	100 g/3½ oz.	200 g/7 oz.	300 g/10½ oz.	400 g/14 oz.
light muscovado sugar	110 g/½ cup packed plus 1 tablespoon	225 g/1 cup packed plus 2 tablespoons	450 g/2¼ cups packed	675 g/3⅓ cups packed	900 g/4½ cups packed
unsalted butter	40 g/3 tablespoons	75 g/5 tablespoons	150 g/1 stick plus 2 tablespoons	225 g/2 sticks	300 g/2½ sticks
large eggs	1	2	4	6	8
vanilla extract	1 teaspoon	2 teaspoons	1 tablespoon	1½ tablespoons	2 tablespoons
salt	a small pinch	a pinch	½ teaspoon	¾ teaspoon	1 teaspoon
plain/all-purpose flour	65 g/½ cup	125 g/1cup	250 g/2 cups	375 g/3 cups	500 g/4 cups
unsweetened cocoa powder	15 g/1 tablespoon	25 g/3 tablespoons	50 g/6 tablespoons	75 g/⅔ cup	100 g/¾ cup
bicarbonate of soda/ baking soda	½ teaspoon	1 teaspoon	2 teaspoons	3 teaspoons	4 teaspoons
baking time	20 minutes	20–25 minutes	25–30 minutes	30–35 minutes	40–45 minutes

For the Rich Chocolate Buttercream

unsalted butter	50 g/3½ tablespoons	100 g/6½ tablespoons	200 g/1 stick plus 5 tablespoons	300 g/2½ sticks	400 g/3 sticks plus 3 tablespoons
icing/confectioners' sugar	90 g/⅔ cup	175 g/1¼ cups	350 g/2½ cups	525 g/3¾ cups	700 g/5 cups
dark chocolate	50 g/1¾ oz.	100 g/3½ oz.	200 g/7 oz.	300 g/10½ oz.	400 g/14 oz.
milk, if needed to slacken	a splash	a splash	a splash	a splash	a splash

For the Red Velvet Cake (to be prepared in 2 shallow cake pans)

INGREDIENTS	15 cm/6 inch round (13 cm/5 inch square)	20 cm/8 inch round (18 cm/7 inch square)	25 cm/10 inch round (23 cm/9 inch square)	30 cm/12 inch round (28 cm/11 inch square)	35 cm/14 inch round (33 cm/13 inch square)
unsalted butter	100 g/6½ tablespoons	200 g/1 stick plus 5 tablespoons	400 g/3 sticks plus 3 tablespoons	600 g/5 sticks plus 2 tablespoons	800 g/7 sticks
(caster) sugar	100 g/½ cup	200 g/1 cup	400 g/2 cups	600 g/3 cups	800 g/4 cups
large eggs	1	2	4	6	8
vanilla extract	½ tablespoon	1 tablespoon	2 tablespoons	3 tablespoons	4 tablespoons
extra-red food colouring paste	1 teaspoon	2 teaspoons	1 tablespoon plus 1 teaspoon	2 tablespoons	2 tablespoons plus 2 teaspoons
buttermilk	125 ml/½ cup	250 ml/1 cup	500 ml/2 cups	750 ml/3 cups	1 litre/4 cups
plain/all-purpose flour	125 g/1 cup	250 g/2 cups	500 g/4 cups	750 g/6 cups	1 kg/8 cups
unsweetened cocoa powder	10 g/1 tablespoon plus 1 teaspoon	20 g/2½ tablespoons	40 g/⅓ cup	60 g/½ cup	80 g/⅔ cup
baking powder	½ teaspoon	1 teaspoon	2 teaspoons	3 teaspoons	4 teaspoons
salt	a pinch	¼ teaspoon	¾ teaspoon	1 teaspoon	1¼ teaspoons
white wine vinegar	1 teaspoon	2 teaspoons	1 tablespoon plus 1 teaspoon	2 tablespoons	2 tablespoons plus 2 teaspoons
bicarbonate of soda/ baking soda	½ teaspoon	1 teaspoon	2 teaspoons	3 teaspoons	4 teaspoons
baking time	20–25 minutes	25–30 minutes	35–40 minutes	40–45 minutes	45–50 minutes

For the Vanilla Cream Cheese Frosting

unsalted butter	50 g/3½ tablespoons	75 g/5 tablespoons	150 g/1 stick plus 2 tablespoons	225 g/2 sticks	300 g/2½ sticks
Philadelphia cream cheese	50 g/3½ tablespoons	75 g/5 tablespoons	150 g/½ cup plus 2 tablespoons	225 g/scant 1 cup	300 g/1¼ cups
icing/confectioners' sugar	200 g/1½ cups less 1 tablespoon	300 g/2 cups plus 2 tablespoons	600 g/4¼ cups	900 g/6½ cups (2 lbs.)	1.2 kg/8½ cups (2 lbs. 10 oz.)
vanilla extract	1 tablespoon	1½ tablespoons	3 tablespoons	4 tablespoons	6 tablespoons

For the Apple and Calvados Cake (to be prepared in 2 shallow cake pans)

INGREDIENTS	15 cm/6 inch round (13 cm/5 inch square)	20 cm/8 inch round (18 cm/7 inch square)	23 cm/9 inch round (20 cm/8 inch square)	25 cm/10 inch round (23 cm/9 inch square)	30 cm/12 inch round (28 cm/11 inch square)
sultanas/golden raisins	50 g/⅓ cup	100 g/⅔ cup	150 g/1 cup	200 g/1⅓ cups	300 g/2 cups
Calvados	90 ml/6 tablespoons	180 ml/¾ cup	270 ml/1 cup plus 2 tablespoons	360 ml/1½ cups	540 ml/2¼ cups
apples	2	4	6	8	12
light muscovado sugar	150 g/¾ cup packed	300 g/1½ cups packed	450 g/2⅓ cups packed	600 g/3 cups packed	900 g/4½ cups packed
self-raising flour	100 g/¾ cup	200 g/1½ cups	300 g/2⅓ cups	400 g/3 cups plus 2 tablespoons	600 g/4⅔ cups
baking powder	1 teaspoon	2 teaspoons	3 teaspoons	4 teaspoons	6 teaspoons
ground almonds	50 g/½ cup	100 g/1 cup	150 g/1½ cups	200 g/2 cups	300 g/3 cups
unsalted butter	150 g/1 stick plus 2 tablespoons	300 g/2½ sticks	450 g/4 sticks	600 g/5 sticks	900 g/8 sticks
large eggs	3	6	9	12	18
grated nutmeg	½ teaspoon	1 teaspoon	1½ teaspoons	2 teaspoons	1 tablespoon
salt	a pinch	¼ teaspoon	⅓ teaspoon	½ teaspoon	¾ teaspoon
milk, if needed to slacken	a splash	a splash	a splash	a splash	a splash
baking time	40–45 minutes	50–55 minutes	55–60 minutes	70–75 minutes	75–85 minutes

For the Butterscotch

light muscovado sugar	25 g/2 tablespoons	100 g/½ cup packed	150 g/¾ cup packed	200 g/1 cup packed	300 g/1½ cups packed
salted butter	15 g/1 tablespoon	25 g/1½ tablespoons	40 g/3 tablespoons	50 g/3½ tablespoons	75 g/5 tablespoons

For the Toffee Buttercream

salted butter	25 g/1½ tablespoons	35 g/2½ tablespoons	50 g/3 tablespoons	75 g/5 tablespoons	100 g/6½ tablespoons
light muscovado sugar	25 g/2 tablespoons	35 g/3 tablespoons	50 g/¼ cup packed	75 g/⅓ cup packed plus 1 tablespoon	100 g/½ cup packed
Calvados	2 tablespoons	3 tablespoons	4 tablespoons	90 ml/⅓ cup	120 ml/½ cup
unsalted butter	75 g/5 tablespoons	100 g/6½ tablespoons	150 g/1 stick plus 2 tablespoons	200 g/1 stick plus 5 tablespoons	300 g/2½ sticks
icing/confectioners' sugar	150 g/1 cup	200 g/1½ cups less 1 tablespoon	300 g/2 cups plus 2 tablespoons	450 g/3¼ cups	600 g/4¼ cups

antique lace

For the Sticky Ginger Cake (to be prepared in 2 shallow cake pans)

INGREDIENTS	10 cm/4 inch round (8 cm/3 inch square)	15 cm/6 inch round (13 cm/5 inch square)	20 cm/8 inch round (18 cm/7 inch square)	25 cm/10 inch round (23 cm/9 inch square)	30 cm/12 inch round (28 cm/11 inch square)
unsalted butter	50 g/3½ tablespoons	100 g/6½ tablespoons	200 g/1 stick plus 5 tablespoons	400 g/3 sticks plus 3 tablespoons	600 g/5 sticks plus 2 tablespoons
molasses sugar	40 g/3 tablespoons	75 g/⅓ cup packed	150 g/¾ cup packed	300 g/1½ cups packed	450 g/2¼ cups packed
golden/light corn syrup	25 ml/1½ tablespoons	45 ml/3 tablespoons	90 ml/⅓ cup	180 ml/¾ cup	270 ml/1 cup plus 2 tablespoons
whole milk	50 ml/3½ tablespoons	100 ml/⅓ cup	200 ml/¾ cup	400 ml/1⅔ cups	600 ml/2½ cups
large eggs	½	1	2	4	6
balls of stem ginger	1½	3	6	12	18
self-raising flour	65 g/½ cup	125 g/1 cup	250 g/2 cups	500 g/4 cups	750 g/6 cups
ground ginger	2 teaspoons	1 tablespoon	2 tablespoons	3½ tablespoons	5 tablespoons
salt	a pinch	¼ teaspoon	½ teaspoon	¾ teaspoon	1 teaspoon
ginger syrup (from the stem ginger jar)*	1 tablespoon	2 tablespoons	4 tablespoons	120 ml/scant ½ cup	180 ml/¾ cup
baking time	20–25 minutes	30–35 minutes	35–40 minutes	45–50 minutes	50–60 minutes

For the Ginger Buttercream

unsalted butter	50 g/3½ tablespoons	75 g/5 tablespoons	100 g/6½ tablespoons	200 g/1 stick plus 5 tablespoons	300 g/2½ sticks
ginger syrup*	2 tablespoons	3 tablespoons	90 ml/6 tablespoons	180 ml/¾ cup	270 ml/1 cup plus 2 tablespoons
icing/confectioners' sugar	100 g/¾ cup	150 g/1 cup	200 g/1½ cups less 1 tablespoon	400 g/3 cups	600 g/4¼ cups

* If you need more syrup than the amount which comes in the jar, simply infuse sugar syrup (caster/granulated sugar heated gently with twice as much water, until dissolved) with peeled ginger root.

For the White Chocolate and Cardamom Cake (to be prepared in 1 deep cake pan)

INGREDIENTS	15 cm/6 inch round (13 cm/5 inch square)	23 cm/9 inch round (20 cm/8 inch square)	30 cm/12 inch round (28 cm/11 inch square)
white chocolate	75 g/2½ oz.	150 g/5½ oz.	300 g/10½ oz.
green cardamom pods	12–15	24–30	48–60
unsalted butter	100 g/6½ tablespoons	200 g/1 stick plus 5 tablespoons	400 g/3 sticks plus 3 tablespoons
(caster) sugar	100 g/½ cup	200 g/1 cup	400 g/2 cups
medium eggs	2	4	8
vanilla extract	½ tablespoon	1 tablespoon	2 tablespoons
self-raising flour	125 g/1 cup	250 g/2 cups	500 g/4 cups
sour cream	75 ml/5 tablespoons	150 ml/⅔ cup	300 ml/1⅓ cups
salt	a pinch	½ teaspoon	1 teaspoon
baking time	30–40 minutes	45–50 minutes	60–70 minutes

For the White Chocolate Buttercream

unsalted butter	100 g/6½ tablespoons	200 g/1 stick plus 5 tablespoons	400 g/3 sticks plus 3 tablespoons
white chocolate	100 g/3½ oz.	200 g/7 oz.	400 g/14 oz.
icing/confectioners' sugar	200 g/1½ cups	400 g/3 cups	800 g/5¾ cups
vanilla extract	½ tablespoon	1 tablespoon	2 tablespoons
milk, if needed to slacken	a splash	a splash	a splash

victoriana

For the Black Forest Cake (to be prepared in 1 deep cake pan)

INGREDIENTS	15 cm/6 inch square (18 cm/7 inch round)	20 cm/8 inch square (23 cm/9 inch round)	25 cm/10 inch square (28 cm/11 inch round)	30 cm/12 inch square (33 cm/13 inch round)	35 cm/14 inch square (38 cm/15 inch round)
large eggs	2	5	10	15	20
salt	a pinch	¼ teaspoon	½ teaspoon	¾ teaspoon	1 teaspoon
(caster) sugar	75 g/6 tablespoons	150 g/¾ cup	300 g/1½ cups	450 g/2¼ cups	600 g/3 cups
unsalted butter	100 g/6½ tablespoons	200 g/1 stick plus 5 tablespoons	400 g/3 sticks plus 3 tablespoons	600 g/5 sticks plus 2 tablespoons	800 g/7 sticks
ground almonds	25 g/¼ cup	50 g/½ cup	100 g/1 cup	150 g/1½ cups	200 g/2 cups
dark chocolate	50 g/1¾ oz.	100 g/3½ oz.	200 g/7 oz.	300 g/10½ oz.	400 g/14 oz.
self-raising flour	40 g/⅓ cup	75 g/⅔ cup	150 g/1¼ cups	225 g/1¾ cups	300 g/2⅓ cups
baking powder	1 teaspoon	2 teaspoons	4 teaspoons	6 teaspoons	8 teaspoons
unsweetened cocoa powder	25 g/3 tablespoons	50 g/6 tablespoons	100 g/¾ cup	150 g/1 cup plus 2 tablespoons	200 g/1½ cups
Kirsch-soaked black cherries (drained weight)	125 g/4½ oz.	250 g/9 oz.	500 g/1 lb. 2 oz.	750 g/1 lb. 10 oz.	1 kg/2 lbs. 4 oz.
Kirsch from the cherry jar	1 tablespoon	2 tablespoons	4 tablespoons	90 ml/6 tablespoons	120 ml/scant ½ cup
baking time	30 minutes	40–45 minutes	60 minutes	70–80 minutes	80–90 minutes

For the Cream Cheese Frosting

unsalted butter	75 g/5 tablespoons	150 g/1 stick plus 2 tablespoons	300 g/2½ sticks	450 g/4 sticks	600 g/5 sticks plus 2 tablespoons
Philadelphia cream cheese	75 g/5 tablespoons	150 g/⅔ cup	300 g/1⅓ cups	450 g/2 cups (1 lb.)	600 g/2⅔ cups (1 lb. 5 oz.)
icing/confectioners' sugar	300 g/2 cups plus 2 tablespoons	600 g/4¼ cups	1.2 kg/8 cups (2 lbs. 12 oz.)	1.8 kg/12 cups (4 lbs.)	2.4 kg/16 cups (5 lbs. 5 oz.)
vanilla extract	½ tablespoon	1 tablespoon	2 tablespoons	3 tablespoons	4 tablespoons

film noir

Quantities are all multiples of the recipe quantities on page 75

midnight lotus

For the Chocolate Rum Truffle Cake (to be prepared in 2 shallow cake pans)

INGREDIENTS	13 cm/5 inch square (15 cm/6 inch round)	20 cm/8 inch square (23 cm/9 inch round)	28 cm/11 inch square (30 cm/12 inch round)
large eggs, separated	4	8	16
whole eggs	1	2	4
salt	a pinch	¼ teaspoon	½ teaspoon
dark muscovado sugar	200 g/1 cup packed	400 g/2 cups packed	800 g/4 cups packed
ground almonds	125 g/1¼ cups	250 g/2½ cups	500 g/5 cups
dark chocolate	200 g/7 oz.	400 g/14 oz.	800 g/1 lb. 12 oz.
dark rum	2 teaspoons	1½ tablespoons	3 tablespoons
baking time	25–30 minutes	30–35 minutes	35–40 minutes

For the Whipped Rum Ganache

dark chocolate	50 g/1¾ oz.	150 g/5½ oz.	300 g/10½ oz.
single/light cream	50 ml/3½ tablespoons	150 ml/⅔ cup	300 ml/1¼ cups
salt	a pinch	¼ teaspoon	½ teaspoon
unsalted butter	25 g/1½ tablespoons	75 g/5 tablespoons	150 g/1 stick plus 2 tablespoons
icing/confectioners' sugar	50 g/generous ⅓ cup	100 g/¾ cup	200 g/1½ cups
dark rum	1½ tablespoons	3 tablespoons	100 ml/⅓ cup

art nouveau

For the Espresso Cake (to be prepared in 1 deep cake pan)

INGREDIENTS	15 cm/6 inch round (13 cm/5 inch square)	20 cm/8 inch round (18 cm/7 inch square)	23 cm/9 inch round (20 cm/8 inch square)	25 cm/10 inch round (23 cm/9 inch square)	30 cm/12 inch round (28 cm/11 inch square)
(caster) sugar	190 g/scant 1 cup	250 g/1¼ cups	375 g/1¾ cups	500 g/2½ cups	750 g/3¾ cups
large eggs	6	8	12	16	24
unsalted butter	40 g/3 tablespoons	50 g/3½ tablespoons	75 g/5 tablespoons	100 g/6½ tablespoons	150 g/1 stick plus 2 tablespoons
instant espresso powder	1 teaspoon	1½ teaspoons	2 teaspoons	1 tablespoon	1½ tablespoons
hot water	2 teaspoons	1 tablespoon	1½ tablespoons	2 tablespoons	3 tablespoons
plain/all-purpose flour	190 g/1½ cups	250 g/2 cups	375 g/3 cups	500 g/4 cups	750 g/6 cups
baking time	20–25 mins	25–30 mins	30–35 mins	35–40 mins	40–45 mins

For the Espresso Buttercream

unsalted butter	75 g/5 tablespoons	100 g/6½ tablespoons	150 g/1 stick plus 2 tablespoons	200 g/1 stick plus 5 tablespoons	300 g/2½ sticks
icing/confectioners' sugar	150 g/1 cup	200 g/1½ cups	300 g/2 cups plus 2 tablespoons	400 g/3 cups	600 g/4¼ cups
instant espresso powder	1 teaspoon	1½ teaspoons	2 teaspoons	1 tablespoon	1½ tablespoons
hot water	2 teaspoons	1 tablespoon	1½ tablespoons	2 tablespoons	3 tablespoons
milk, if needed to slacken	a splash	a splash	a splash	a splash	a splash

something borrowed...

Quantities are all multiples of the recipe quantities on page 91.

vintage rose

For the Vanilla Cupcakes or a Tier of Vanilla Sponge (to be prepared in 2 shallow cake pans)

INGREDIENTS	12 cupcakes (15 cm/6 inch round or 13 cm/5 inch square)	24 cupcakes (20 cm/8 inch round or 18 cm/7 inch square)	48 cupcakes (25 cm/10 inch round or 23 cm/9 inch square)	96 cupcakes (30 cm/12 inch round or 28 cm/11 inch square)
unsalted butter	100 g/6½ tablespoons	200 g/1 stick plus 5 tablespoons	400 g/3 sticks plus 3 tablespoons	800 g/7 sticks
(caster) sugar	100 g/½ cup	200 g/1 cup	400 g/2 cups	800 g/4 cups
large eggs	2	4	8	16
self-raising flour	100 g/¾ cup	200 g/1½ cups	400 g/3 cups plus 2 tablespoons	800 g/6½ cups
baking powder	½ teaspoon	1 teaspoon	2 teaspoons	4 teaspoons
vanilla extract	2 teaspoons	1½ tablespoons	3 tablespoons	6 tablespoons
milk, if needed to slacken	a splash	a splash	a splash	a splash
baking time for cupcakes	15–20 minutes	15–20 minutes	15–20 minutes	15–20 minutes
baking times for large cakes	15–20 minutes	20–25 minutes	25–30 minutes	35–40 minutes

For the Vanilla Buttercream

unsalted butter	75 g/5 tablespoons	125 g/1 stick plus 1 tablespoon	250 g/2¼ sticks	500 g/4½ sticks
icing/confectioners' sugar	150 g/1 cup	250 g/1¾ cups	500 g/3⅔ cups	1 kg/7¼ cups
vanilla extract	2 teaspoons	1½ tablespoons	3 tablespoons	6 tablespoons
milk, if needed to slacken	a splash	a splash	a splash	a splash

For the Carrot Cake (to be prepared in 2 shallow cake pans)

INGREDIENTS	15 cm/6 inch round (13 cm/5 inch square)	20 cm/8 inch round (18 cm/7 inch square)	23 cm/9 inch round (20 cm/8 inch square)	25 cm/10 inch round (23 cm/9 inch square)	30 cm/12 inch round (28 cm/11 inch square)
sultanas/golden raisins	75 g/½ cup	115 g/¾ cup	150 g/1 cup	225 g/1½ cups	300 g/2 cups
large oranges	1	1½	2	3	4
large eggs	2	3	4	6	8
sunflower oil	150 ml/⅔ cup	225 ml/scant 1 cup	300 ml/1¼ cups	450 ml/2 cups less 2 tablespoons	600 ml/2½ cups
light muscovado sugar	200 g/1 cup packed	300 g/1½ cups packed	400 g/2 cups packed	600 g/3 cups packed	800 g/4 cups packed
grated carrot	250 g/1¼ cups	375 g/1¾ cups	500 g/2½ cups	750 g/3½ cups	1 kilo/5 cups
roughly chopped pecan nuts (optional)	75 g/¾ cup	115 g/generous 1 cup	150 g/1½ cups	225 g/2¼ cups	300 g/3 cups
self-raising flour	175 g/1⅓ cups	265 g/2 cups	350 g/3 cups	525 g/4¼ cups	700 g/5½ cups
bicarbonate of soda/ baking soda	1 teaspoon	1½ teaspoons	2 teaspoons	3 teaspoons	4 teaspoons
grated nutmeg	½ teaspoon	¾ teaspoon	1 teaspoon	1½ teaspoons	2 teaspoons
ground cinnamon	2 teaspoons	1 tablespoon	1 tablespoon plus 1 teaspoon	1 tablespoon plus 2 teaspoons	2 tablespoons
mixed/apple-pie spice	1 teaspoon	1½ teaspoons	2 teaspoons	1 tablespoon	1½ tablespoons
salt	a pinch	¼ teaspoon	½ teaspoon	¾ teaspoon	1 teaspoon
baking time	35–40 minutes	45–50 minutes	50–60 minutes	60–70 minutes	80–90 minutes

For the Lemon Cream Cheese Icing

Philadelphia cream cheese	125 g/½ cup	185 g/¾ cup	250 g/1 cup	350 g/1⅓ cups	500 g/2 cups
unsalted butter	75 g/5 tablespoons	115 g/1 stick	150 g/1 stick plus 2 tablespoons	225 g/2 sticks	300 g/2½ sticks
juice of lemons	1	1½	2	3	4
icing/confectioners' sugar	300 g/2 cups plus 2 tablespoons	400 g/3 cups	600 g/4¼ cups	900 g/6½ cups	1.2 kg/8 cups (2 lbs. 12 oz.)

brighton rock

For the Peanut Butter and Chocolate Chip Cake (to be prepared in 2 shallow cake pans)

INGREDIENTS	15 cm/6 inch round (13 cm/5 inch square)	20 cm/8 inch round (18 cm/7 inch square)	23 cm/9 inch round (20 cm/8 inch square)	25 cm/10 inch round (23 cm/9 inch square)	30 cm/12 inch round (28 cm/11 inch square)
unsalted butter	65 g/4½ tablespoons	135 g/1 stick plus 1 tablespoon	200 g/1 stick plus 5 tablespoons	265 g/2 sticks plus 2 tablespoons	400 g/3 sticks plus 3 tablespoons
smooth peanut butter	35 g/2½ tablespoons	65 g/4½ tablespoons	100 g/scant ½ cup	135 g/½ cup plus 1½ tablespoons	200 g/1 cup less 2 tablespoons
(caster) sugar	100 g/½ cup	200 g/1 cup	300 g/1½ cups	400 g/2 cups	600 g/3 cups
large eggs	2	4	6	8	12
self-raising flour	100 g/¾ cup	200 g/1½ cups	300 g/2⅓ cups	400 g/3 cups plus 2 tablespoons	600 g/4⅔ cups
baking powder	1 teaspoon	1½ teaspoons	2 teaspoons	3 teaspoons	4 teaspoons
salt	a pinch	¼ teaspoon	½ teaspoon	¾ teaspoon	1 teaspoon
vanilla extract	1 teaspoon	2 teaspoons	1 tablespoon	1½ tablespoons	2 tablespoons
dark chocolate chips	75 g/½ cup	100 g/⅔ cup	150 g/1 cup	200 g/1⅓ cups	300 g/2 cups
baking time	20–25 minutes	25–30 minutes	30–35 minutes	35–40 minutes	40–45 minutes

For the Chocolate and Peanut Buttercream

unsalted butter	35 g/2½ tablespoons	50 g/3½ tablespoons	75 g/5 tablespoons	100 g/6½ tablespoons	150 g/1 stick plus 2 tablespoons
smooth peanut butter	35 g/2½ tablespoons	50 g/3½ tablespoons	75 g/5 tablespoons	100 g/scant ½ cup	150 g/⅔ cup
icing/confectioners' sugar	140 g/1 cup	200 g/1½ cups	300 g/2 cups plus 2 tablespoons	400 g/3 cups	600 g/4¼ cups
dark chocolate	35 g/1¼ oz.	50 g/1¾ oz.	75 g/2¾ oz.	100 g/3½ oz.	150 g/5½ oz.
milk, if needed to slacken	a splash	a splash	a splash	a splash	a splash

jade garden

For the Orange Polenta Cake (to be prepared in 1 deep cake pan)

INGREDIENTS	15 cm/6 inch round (13 cm/5 inch square)	20 cm/8 inch round (18 cm/7 inch square)	23 cm/9 inch round (20 cm/8 inch square)	25 cm/10 inch round (23 cm/9 inch square)	30 cm/12 inch round (28 cm/11 inch square)
polenta/cornmeal	175 g/1⅓ cups	260 g/2 cups	350 g/2¾ cups	525 g/4 cups	700 g/5½ cups
plain/all-purpose flour	50 g/6 tablespoons	75 g/⅔ cup	100 g/¾ cup	150 g/1¼ cups	200 g/1½ cups
baking powder	1 teaspoon	2 teaspoons	3 teaspoons	4 teaspoons	5 teaspoons
salt	a pinch	¼ teaspoon	⅓ teaspoon	½ teaspoon	1 teaspoon
oranges	1	2	3	4	6
plain yogurt	75 ml/5 tablespoons	110 ml/scant ½ cup	150 ml/⅔ cup	220 ml/1 cup less 2 tablespoons	300 ml/1¼ cups
sunflower oil	75 ml/5 tablespoons	110 ml/scant ½ cup	150 ml/⅔ cup	220 ml/1 cup less 2 tablespoons	300 ml/1¼ cups
large whole eggs	2	3	4	6	8
large egg whites	2	3	4	6	8
(caster) sugar	200 g/1 cup	300 g/1½ cups	400 g/2 cups	600 g/3 cups	800 g/4 cups
(caster) sugar for syrup	50 g/¼ cup	75 g/⅓ cup	100 g/½ cup	150 g/¾ cup	200 g/1 cup
baking time	40–45 minutes	45–50 minutes	55–60 minutes	60–70 minutes	80–90 minutes

summer fete

For the Lemon Drizzle Cake (to be prepared in 1 deep cake pan)

INGREDIENTS	15 cm/6 inch round (13 cm/5 inch square)	20 cm/8 inch round (18 cm/7 inch square)	25 cm/10 inch round (23 cm/9 inch square)	30 cm/12 inch round (28 cm/11 inch square)	35 cm/14 inch round (33 cm/13 inch square)
unsalted butter	100 g/6½ tablespoons	200 g/1 stick plus 5 tablespoons	400 g/3 sticks plus 3 tablespoons	600 g/5 sticks plus 5 tablespoons	800 g/7 sticks
(caster) sugar	150 g/¾ cup	300 g/1½ cups	600 g/3 cups	800 g/4 cups	1.2 kg/6 cups (2 lbs. 10 oz.)
self-raising flour	150 g/1¼ cups	300 g/2⅓ cups	600 g/4⅔ cups	800 g/6½ cups	1.2 kg/9½ cups (2 lbs. 10 oz.)
baking powder	1 teaspoon	2 teaspoons	4 teaspoons	6 teaspoons	8 teaspoons
large eggs	2	4	8	12	16
whole milk	60 ml/¼ cup	120 ml/scant ½ cup	240 ml/scant 1 cup	360 ml/1½ cups	480 ml/2 cups
lemons	2	4	8	12	16
(caster) sugar for drizzle	100 g/½ cup	200 g/1 cup	400 g/2 cups	600 g/3 cups	800 g/4 cups
lemon curd	45 g/3 tablespoons	60 g/4 tablespoons	90 g/6 tablespoons	120 g/½ cup	180 g/¾ cup
baking time	30–35 minutes	40–45 minutes	50–55 minutes	75–85 minutes	80–95 minutes

spring flowers

For the Green Tea Cake (to be prepared in 2 shallow cake pans)

INGREDIENTS	15 cm/6 inch round (13 cm/5 inch square)	20 cm/8 inch round (18 cm/7 inch square)	25 cm/10 inch round (23 cm/9 inch square)	30 cm/12 inch round (28 cm/11 inch square)	35 cm/14 inch round (33 cm/13 inch square)
unsalted butter	100 g/6½ tablespoons	200 g/1 stick plus 5 tablespoons	400 g/3 sticks plus 3 tablespoons	600 g/5 sticks plus 2 tablespoons	800 g/7 sticks
(caster) sugar	100 g/½ cup	200 g/1 cup	400 g/2 cups	600 g/3 cups	800 g/4 cups
large eggs	2	4	8	12	16
self-raising flour	75 g/⅔ cup	150 g/1¼ cups	300 g/2⅓ cups	450 g/3⅓ cups	600 g/4⅔ cups
baking powder	1 teaspoon	2 teaspoons	4 teaspoons	6 teaspoons	8 teaspoons
ground almonds	25 g/¼ cup	50 g/½ cup	100 g/1 cup	150 g/1½ cups	200 g/2 cups
matcha powder	1 tablespoon	2 tablespoons	40 g/¼ cup	60 g/generous ⅓ cup	80 g/½ cup
milk, if needed to slacken	a splash	a splash	a splash	a splash	a splash
baking time	20–25 minutes	25–30 minutes	30–35 minutes	35–40 minutes	45–50 minutes

For the Ginger Buttercream

unsalted butter	35 g/2½ tablespoons	75 g/5 tablespoons	150 g/1 stick plus 2 tablespoons	225 g/2 sticks	300 g/2½ sticks
icing/confectioners' sugar	100 g/¾ cup	200 g/1½ cups	400 g/3 cups	600 g/4¼ cups	800 g/5¾ cups
ginger syrup	1–2 tablespoons	2–3 tablespoons	4–5 tablespoons	90–120 ml/⅓–½ cup	120–150 ml/½–⅔ cup
Philadelphia cream cheese	15 g/1 tablespoon	25 g/1½ tablespoons	50 g/3½ tablespoons	75 g/5 tablespoons	100 g/6½ tablespoons
balls of stem ginger,	1	2	4	6	8

autumn hedgerow

For the Fruits of the Forest Torte (to be prepared in 2 shallow cake pans)

INGREDIENTS	13 cm/5 inch round (10 cm/4 inch square)	18 cm/7 inch round (15 cm/6 inch square)	23 cm/9 inch round (20 cm/8 inch square)	28 cm/11 inch round (25 cm/10 inch square)
eggs	3 medium	5 large	8 large	12 large
(caster) sugar	60 g/⅓ cup	120 g/⅔ cup	200 g/1 cup	300 g/1½ cups
ground almonds	90 g/scant 1 cup	180 g/1¾ cups	300 g/3 cups	450 g/4½ cups
white chocolate	90 g/3¼ oz.	180 g/6¼ oz.	300 g/10½ oz.	450 g/1 lb.
raspberry purée	60 ml/¼ cup	120 ml/½ cup	200 ml/¾ cup	300 ml/1¼ cups
blackcurrant purée	60 ml/¼ cup	120 ml/½ cup	200 ml/¾ cup	300 ml/1¼ cups
blackberry purée	25 ml/1½ tablespoons	60 ml/¼ cup	100 ml/⅓ cup plus 1 tablespoon	150 ml/⅔ cup
salt	a pinch	¼ teaspoon	½ teaspoon	¾ teaspoon
baking time	30–35 minutes	35–40 minutes	45–50 minutes	55–60 minutes

For the Berry Ganache

dark chocolate	60 g/2¼ oz.	120 g/4¼ oz.	200 g/7 oz.	300 g/10½ oz.
unsalted butter	60 g/½ stick	120 g/1 stick	200 g/1 stick plus 5 tablespoons	300 g/2½ sticks
fruit purée (mixture of raspberry, blackberry and blackcurrant)	60 ml/¼ cup	120 ml/½ cup	200 ml/¾ cup	300 ml/1¼ cups
double/heavy cream	60 ml/¼ cup	120 ml/½ cup	200 ml/¾ cup	300 ml/1¼ cups
light muscovado sugar	20 g/1½ tablespoons	40 g/3 tablespoons	75 g/⅓ cup packed plus 1 tablespoon	115 g/½ cup packed plus 1 tablespoon

winter wonderland

For the Chestnut Cake (to be prepared in 2 shallow cake pans)

INGREDIENTS	15 cm/6 inch round (13 cm/5 inch square)	23 cm/9 inch round (20 cm/8 inch square)	30 cm/12 inch round (28 cm/11 inch square)
(caster) sugar	50 g/¼ cup	100 g/½ cup	200 g/1 cup
runny honey	50 g/3½ tablespoons	100 g/6½ tablespoons	200 g/¾ cup
large eggs	4	8	16
unsalted butter	40 g/3 tablespoons	75 g/5 tablespoons	150 g/1 stick plus 2 tablespoons
ground hazelnuts	50 g/⅓ cup	100 g/⅔ cup	200 g/1⅓ cups
chestnut flour	50 g/scant ½ cup	100 g/¾ cup plus 2 tablespoons	200 g/1⅔ cups
salt	a pinch	¼ teaspoon	½ teaspoon
baking time	35–40 mins	45–50 mins	60–70 minutes

For the Chestnut Frosting

	15 cm/6 inch round	23 cm/9 inch round	30 cm/12 inch round
unsalted butter	40 g/3 tablespoons	75 g/5 tablespoons	150 g/1 stick plus 2 tablespoons
Philadelphia cream cheese	40 g/3 tablespoons	75 g/5 tablespoons	150 g/⅔ cup
chestnut purée*	250 g/9 oz.	500 g/1 lb. 2 oz.	1kg/2 lbs. 4 oz.
icing/confectioners' sugar	200 g/1½ cups	400 g/3 cups	800 g/5¾ cups

* Follow the recipe on page 136 or buy ready-made sweetened chestnut purée.

covering cakes and drums

Quantities of marzipan/modelling chocolate needed to cover cakes

Cake size		Quantity of marzipan/ modelling chocolate
Round	Square	
10 cm/4 inch	8 cm/3 inch	350 g/12 oz.
13 cm/5 inch	10 cm/4 inch	450 g/1 lb.
15 cm/6 inch	13 cm/5 inch	550 g/1 lb. 4 oz.
18 cm/7 inch	15 cm/6 inch	675 g/1 lb. 8 oz.
20 cm/8 inch	18 cm/7 inch	775 g/1 lb. 11 oz.
23 cm/9 inch	20 cm/8 inch	875 g/ 1 lb. 15 oz.
25 cm/10 inch	23 cm/9 inch	1 kg/2 lbs. 4 oz.
28 cm/11 inch	25 cm/10 inch	1.25 kg/2 lbs. 12 oz.
30 cm/12 inch	28 cm/11 inch	1.5 kg/3 lbs. 5 oz.
33 cm/13 inch	30 cm/12 inch	1.75 kg/3 lbs. 14 oz.
35 cm/14 inch	33 cm/13 inch	2 kg/4 lbs. 8 oz.

Quantities of sugar paste needed to cover cakes

Cake size		Quantity of sugar paste
Round	Square	
5 cm/2 inch	2.5 cm/1 inch	200 g/7 oz.
8 cm/3 inch	5 cm/2 inch	300 g/10 oz.
10 cm/4 inch	8 cm/3 inch	400 g/14 oz.
13 cm/5 inch	10 cm/4 inch	500 g/1 lb. 2 oz.
15 cm/6 inch	13 cm/5 inch	625 g/1 lb. 6 oz.
18 cm/7 inch	15 cm/6 inch	750 g/1 lb. 10 oz.
20 cm/8 inch	18 cm/7 inch	850 g/1 lb. 14 oz.
23 cm/9 inch	20 cm/8 inch	1 kg/2 lbs. 4 oz.
25 cm/10 inch	23 cm/9 inch	1.25 kg/2 lbs. 12 oz.
28 cm/11 inch	25 cm/10 inch	1.5 kg/3 lbs. 5 oz.
30 cm/12 inch	28 cm/11 inch	1.85 kg/4 lbs.
33 cm/13 inch	30 cm/12 inch	2.25 kg/5 lbs.
35 cm/14 inch	33 cm/13 inch	2.5 kg/5 lbs. 8 oz.

Quantities of sugar paste/modelling chocolate needed to cover cake drums

Cake size		Quantity of sugar paste/ modelling chocolate
Round	Square	
15 cm/6 inch	13 cm/5 inch	250 g/9 oz.
18 cm/7 inch	15 cm/6 inch	350 g/12 oz.
20 cm/8 inch	18 cm/7 inch	500 g/1 lb. 2 oz.
23 cm/9 inch	20 cm/8 inch	650 g/1 lb. 7 oz.
25 cm/10 inch	23 cm/9 inch	750 g/1 lb. 10 oz.
28 cm/11 inch	25 cm/10 inch	850 g/1 lb. 14 oz.
30 cm/12 inch	28 cm/11 inch	950 g/2 lbs. 2 oz.
33 cm/13 inch	30 cm/12 inch	1.05 kg/2 lbs. 6 oz.
35 cm/14 inch	33 cm/13 inch	1.15 kg/2 lbs. 9 oz.
38 cm/15 inch	35 cm/14 inch	1.25 kg/2 lbs. 12 oz.
40 cm/16 inch	38 cm/15 inch	1.35 kg/3 lbs.
43 cm/17 inch	40 cm/16 inch	1.5 kg/3 lbs. 5 oz.

stockists and suppliers

UK

Cake Craft World
Large stockist of general cake decorating supplies, from sugar paste, modelling chocolate and edible ink pens, to heavy-duty boxes and non-stick mats for safely transporting your cakes.
Tel: 01732 46 35 73
www.cakecraftworld.co.uk

The Cake Decorating Company
Shop and online retailer of a large selection of cake decorating materials, including the birdcage stencil (see page 102).
2b Triumph Road
Nottingham, NG7 2GA
Tel: 0115 822 4521
www.thecakedecoratingcompany.co.uk

FUNKIN
Online stockists of 100% natural fruit purées, including all those required for the Fruits of the Forest Torte on page 130.
Tel: 020 7328 4440
www.funkin.co.uk

Home and Pantry
For beautiful cake stands, candles, plates and trinkets.
114 Islington High Street
Camden Passage
London, N1 8EG
Tel: 020 7226 9528
www.homeandpantry.com

Jane Asher
Online retailer and London shop stocking a huge selection of baking and sugarcraft supplies. Ship worldwide.
22–24 Cale Street
London, SW3 3QU
Tel: 020 7584 6177
www.janeasher.com

Kleins
Online retailer and London shop stocking a large selection of ribbons.
5 Noel Street
London, W1F 8GD
Tel: 020 7437 6162
www.kleins.co.uk

Shipton Mill
Specialist flour mill that stocks a huge range of flours, including chestnut. Buy online, through selected retailers or at the mill itself.
Long Newnton
Tetbury
Gloucestershire, GL8 8RP
Tel: 01666 505050
www.shipton-mill.com

Squires Kitchen
Large retailer of cake decorating and sugarcraft supplies, including food-grade gold leaf. Buy online or visit their shop.
Squires House
3 Waverley Lane
Farnham
Surrey, GU9 8BB
Tel: 0845 225 5671
www.squires-shop.com

Style Workshop
Leading florists that will supply posies for the top of your wedding cakes.
39 High Street
Tunbridge Wells
Kent, TN1 1XL
Tel: 01892 529 353
www.styleworkshop.co.uk

Flowers at Colonnade
Beautiful flowers with next day national and worldwide delivery.
10 Monson Road
Tunbridge Wells
Kent, TN1 1ND
Tel: 08000 935 193
www.colonnadeflorist.co.uk

US

Kitchen Krafts
A large range of square and round pans in different sizes, as well as decorating tools and edible decorations.
Tel: 800 298 5389
www.kitchenkrafts.com

N.Y. Cake
Online retailer and New York store stocking a huge range of specialist cake decorating equipment, including icing in a large selection of colours and the birdcage stencil (see page 102).
56 West 22nd Street
Between 5th and 6th Avenues
New York, NY 10010
Tel: 800 942 2539
www.nycake.com

Sugarcraft
Every type of cake decoration imaginable, including a huge range of ready to roll coloured icing and ribbons to go around your cake.
www.sugarcraft.com

Sur la Table
Chain of stores (check the website for your nearest store) and online retailer of a large range of cake decorating supplies, including bakeware, piping bags and decorating tools.
www.surlatable.com

Wilton
The site to browse for all manner of baking and decorating supplies, from edibles and decorating tools, to sturdy boxes for transporting the cake to the reception.
www.wilton.com

index

acknowledgments

A special thanks must go to my amazing mum, Lesley, for first teaching me to bake and for her continued and unwavering support while I have built up this business. Huge and heartfelt thanks must also go to my gorgeous partner, Richard: thank you for all your help and encouragement and for never failing to make me laugh.

A big hug of thanks must go to my dad, uncle, my three sisters, my nephews and my brothers-in-law, for all being such committed testers of new cake flavours over the years. A special thanks to Sam for all your help with mood boards and for being dragged around Angel shopping for props – I couldn't have done it without you!

I would also like to thank the amazing team I've had the privilege of working with on this book. Thanks to Laura Forrester for the stunning photography. Your talent, humour and friendship helped make the shoots a total joy. Thank you, Luis Peral, for all your passion and commitment, and for introducing me to the concept of Barbie doll cakes! A special thanks to Rebecca Woods for your patience, kindness and all your outstanding hard work in orchestrating this project, and to Julia Charles and Leslie Harrington for your invaluable input and for being such charming, lovely ladies. Many thanks to Barbara Zuñiga for designing such a beautiful layout and also to Jack Flynn, Danny Lillie, Stephen Rasmusen, Karl Donovan and Miriam Nice for your stellar work assisting at the photo shoots. The days wouldn't have been nearly as much fun or productive without you all. Special thanks must go to my agent, Olivia Guest, for having so much faith in me and faith in my writing.

Thanks to *The Spa Hotel* in Tunbridge Wells (www.spahotel.co.uk) for allowing us to use your beautiful rooms and grounds, *The Style Workshop* for the stunning flowers you donated for our photography, *Flowers at Colonnade* for giving us a generous discount, *Laura Ashley* for providing us with exquisite wallpapers and *Home and Pantry* for lending us your gorgeous wares. Thank you all for helping us to create such beautiful images.

Heartfelt thanks to Beth and Amanda for keeping things ticking over at *VCB* HQ while I've been writing this book and, finally, thanks must go to my army of test bakers. There are too many of you to name individually, but your weighing, whisking and baking results have been invaluable. Thank you.

For Rosie and George, my late beloved grandparents. Two of the warmest and funniest people I have ever had the privilege to know, and two of the most enthusiastic cake eaters I have ever met.